THE TRON THEATRE COMPANY, GLASGOW

present

SAN DIEGO

Written by David Greig
Directed by Marisa Zanotti and David Greig
Designed by Simon Vincenzi

A co-production with the Edinburgh International Festival

SAN DIEGO
was originally staged in August 200(
by the Tron Theatre Company in a co-pro
with the Edinburgh International Fest
at the Royal Lyceum Theatre, Edinbu

The text as published here represents the version
used for the start of rehearsals for the Tron Theatr

The Cast

BILLY BOYD	David Greig
CALLUM CUTHBERTSON	Pious/David in Consultancy
ABIGAIL DAVIES	Laura
HUSS GARBIYA	David the Patient
TAMZIN GRIFFIN	Counsellor/Woman on Phone/ Mother Superior/Patience
TONY GUILFOYLE	The Pilot
PAUL THOMAS HICKEY	Innocent/The Bedouin Tribesman/ David in Consultancy
VICKI LIDDELLE	Marie/San Diego Cop
MILTON LOPES	Daniel
NICHOLAS PINNOCK	Andrew/San Diego Cop/ David in Consultancy
GABRIEL QUIGLEY	Stewardess/Amy (Hooker)/ Sarah

The Team

Co-director	Marisa Zanotti
Co-director	David Greig
Designer	Simon Vincenzi
Lighting Designer	Chahine Yavroyan
Sound Designer	Graeme Miller
Producer for the Tron Theatre	Neil Murray
Production Manager	Jo Masson
Technical Manager	Malcolm Rogan
Technician	Iain Urquhart
Technician	Mark Hughes
Company Stage Manager	Peter Screen
Deputy Stage Manager	Kirsty Paton
Assistant Stage Manager	Alison Brodie
Assistant Stage Manager	Jacqueline Hume
Wardrobe Supervisor	Anne Matheson
Wardrobe Assistant	Katie Todd
Scenic Artist	Julie Kirsop
Fight Director	Alison de Burgh
Placement	Nicola Hill
Placement	Claire Smith
Set Construction	J & B Scenery

BILLY BOYD
(David Greig)

On the stage Billy has performed in various UK
productions including *The Ballad of Crazy Paola*,
by Arne Sierens, *The Speculator, An Experienced
Woman Gives Advice, Therese Raquin, Britannia
Rules, Kill the Old Torture Their Young, The Chic
Nerds, Much Ado About Nothing, The Merchant of
Venice, Trainspotting, Merlin the Magnificent* and
The Slab Boys. His screen credits include *Coming
Soon, Chapter and Verse, Urban Ghost Story, Soldier's Leap, Sniper 470*,
the *Lord of the Rings* trilogy, *Master and Commander*, and *The Far Side
of the World*.

CALLUM CUTHBERTSON
(Pious/David in Consultancy)

Callum's recent theatre work has included *King
Matt, Doctor Korczak's Example* and *The Good
Woman of Setzuan* (TAG); *News at When, 24 Hours,
A Little Rain* (7:84); *Lament, Mainstream* and
Casanova (Suspect Culture); *Love Freaks* and
The Coach (Tron); and *Passing Places, Lazy Bed,
Danny 306* and *First Bites* (Traverse). Film, TV and
radio credits include *The Commuter* (BBC Radio
Scotland); *Rockface, Rab C Nesbitt, Ruffian Hearts* and *English Express*
(all BBC); *High Road* (STV); *Breaking the Waves* (Zeotrope Films). Callum
has also written two award-winning short films.

ABIGAIL DAVIES
(Laura)

Abigail has appeared on stage as Sybil in Noël
Coward's *Private Lives* (Volcano Theatre),
and as Julia in *I Am Dandy* (David Gale Ensemble).
On television her roles have included parts in
Lenny Blue (Granada) and *The Bill* (Thames).
She has also played Zoe in *Beneath the Skin* for
BBC Radio 4.

HUSS GARBIYA
(David the Patient)

Huss' theatre credits include *Transmissions*, *Ash Girl* and *Quarantine* (Birmingham Rep), *Made of Stone* (Royal Court Theatre), *Wise Guys* (Contact Theatre, Manchester), *The Loneliness of the Long Distance Runner* (Nottingham Playhouse), *Solomon and the Big Cat* (Nuffield Theatre), *Peter Pan* and *Runners* (Sheffield Crucible Theatre).

For film and television Huss has made appearances in *Clocking Off* (Granada), *Buried* (World Productions), *Victoria* (Ideal World), *The Bill* (Pearson), *Holby City* and *Eastenders* (BBC), *Some Voices* (Dragon Pictures), *Extremely Dangerous* (Patagonia Films) and the Short Film *Dependence*.

TAMZIN GRIFFIN
(Counsellor/Woman on Phone/
Mother Superior/Patience)

Tamzin is the actress, deviser and writer who plays the female roles in *Shockheaded Peter*, which she helped to create and which enjoyed sell-out runs on/off Broadway, throughout the States and Europe and in the West End. The show won the 2002 Olivier Award for Best Entertainment. She starred in *Red Demon* at the Young Vic earlier this year, directed by Hideki Noda, and she recently finished a run at the Gate Theatre in Celia Parkert's monologue piece *Witness* (2003's Translations Award winner). Tamzin wrote and performed for Channel 4's Emmy Award-winning *Smack the Pony*; stars in Bollywood hit, *Kabhi Khushi Kabhie Gham*; appears in Alex De Rakoff's new film, *The Calcium Kid*; and works regularly with Forced Entertainment. She recorded an animation for Channel 4, *Rolf's Animal Hairdressers*, and has just filmed a pilot for the BBC: *Roadrunner*. She is also the writer and performer of The Funny Lady on the *Teletubbies*, telling tales of the naughty sock, the bad bee and such.

Other performances and installation projects include Semblance's *Obituary* (ICA) and *The Lights Are On . . .* (Royal Court); The Handsome Foundation's *Legend*; *The Fear Show* (ICA, CCA) and Stephen Taylor Woodrow's *Going by Byes*.

She almost played the cello on Baby Bird's album, *Ugly Beautiful*.

TONY GUILFOYLE
(The Pilot)

Tony is currently working on his third collaboration with Robert Lepage, a reworking of the *Dragon's Trilogy*, the others being *The Geometry of Miracles* and *Kindertotenleider*. Previous credits include *The Iceman Cometh* and the *L.A. Plays*, both for the Almeida Theatre; *Shopping and Fucking* at the Geilgud and Queens Theatres and internationally, including the Edinburgh Festival; *The Queen and I* for the Royal Court/Out of Joint Companies; Pasolini's *Teorema* for the Opera della Roma; and, for the RSC, *Outskirts* by Hanif Kureishi.

Tony has extensive experience in experimental, regional and political theatre including Joint Stock, 7:84, and Monstrous Regiment.

His television work has included *The Murder of Stephen Lawrence* and the second series of *Father Ted*, while in film he has played the lead in *The Return* for Film on Four.

Work in Scotland includes *The Sleep* and *Imitation of Life* by Pete Brooks at Glasgow's Mayfest.

PAUL THOMAS HICKEY
(Innocent/Bedouin Tribesman/
David in Consultancy)

Paul trained at the Royal Scottish Academy of Music and Drama in Glasgow. His theatre work has included *The Entertainer* (Citizens' Theatre); *Gagarin Way*, *Green Field*, *Passing Places*, *The Architect* and *Olga* (all at the Traverse); *AD*, *Macbeth*, *Ecstasy*, *One Flew Over the Cuckoo's Nest*, *Still Life* and *Wasted* (all Raindog); *The Backroom* (Bush/Soho Theatre Company); *Mainstream* and *Timeless* (Suspect Culture); *Snatch* (Soho Theatre Company); *Crave* (Paines Plough); *Shining Souls* (Old Vic); *The Slab Boys Trilogy* (Young Vic); *Jump the Life to Come* and *A Night of Gentle Sex Comedies* (7:84 Theatre Company); and *Sailmaker* and *Twelfth Night* (TAG).

On television he has appeared in two series of *Tinsel Town* (BBC Scotland); *Nightlife*, *Cardiac Arrest*, *The Jacobites*, and *Sweetest Feeling* (all BBC); *Taggart*, *The High Road* and *Britoil Fraud* (STV). His film credits include *California Sunshine* and *Wanting and Getting* (both from Zigma Films) and *Charmed* (EVTC).

VICKI LIDDELLE (Marie/San Diego Cop)

Vicki's theatre credits include *Casanova* (Suspect Culture), *Passing Places* (Greenwich Theatre/ Derby Playhouse), *Gravity* (Edinburgh International Festival), *Twelfth Night* (Brunton Theatre), *King of the Fields* (Traverse Theatre), *The Snow Queen* and *Britannia Rules* (both Royal Lyceum, Edinburgh), *Merlin the Magnificent* (Macrobert Arts Centre), *The Suicide* and *Portrait of a Woman* (both Communicado), *Shanghaied* (Nippy Sweeties), *Pinocchio* (Visible

Fictions), *The Glass Menagerie* (Dundee Rep.), *The Happiest Days of Our Lives* (Perth Rep.), *The Prime of Miss Jean Brodie* (The Theatre of Comedy), and *Night Sky* (Stellar Quines).

Her film and television credits include *The Big Tease* (Ideal World / Warner Brothers), *Around Scotland* (BBC Scotland), and *Masterclass with Richard Wilson* (BBC2). Vicki has also worked extensively on radio in *The Mystic Life*; *Rob Roy*; *Adam Bede*; *God's Gift*; *Mercury, Sulphur and Salt*; *McLevy*; *Still Waters*; and *Tally's Blood* (all for BBC Radio 4); *Stop, Think, Wonder* (BBC Radio 3); and *Bondagers*; *The Laughing Policeman*; *The Prime of Miss Jean Brodie*; *Anna Karenina*; *The Swithering Gull*; *Out of the Blue*; *Millennium Tales*; and *Storyline* (all for BBC Radio Scotland).

MILTON LOPES (Daniel)

Milton Lopes was born on the 29th June 1977 in Cape Vert, a Portuguese ex-colony in Africa which became independent in 1974. He emigrated with his family in 1980 to Portugal looking for a better life. They lived in Almada, a town situated in the south side of the Tejo river, near Lisbon, Portugal's capital. He started doing theatre at the age of seventeen, in an amateur company, and two years later he went to the University of Évora, where he graduated in Theatre Studies. There he was the university theatre company's director. Five years later he began teaching drama classes and working as an actor in small independent theatre productions in Lisbon and in Almada. Nowadays he continues to participate in theatre plays, cinema and television shows including, in theatre, *Duck Variations* by David Mamet (directed by Marlos Barbosa) and *Tiestes* by Seneca (directed by Miguel Lintra); on TV, *Saber Amar* (English title, *In Love*); and, in film, *O Delfim* (directed by Fernando Lopes), for which he won the Best Actor Award at the Angra Do Heroísmo International Film Festival, *Um Homem Nao É Um Gato* (TV movie directed by Marie Brand), and *O Jogo Da Glória* (directed by Fernando Vendrell).

NICHOLAS PINNOCK
(Andrew/San Diego Cop/David in Consultancy)

Born in London, Nicholas started his acting career aged twelve at Hammersmith's Corona Academy stage school. After working on numerous television programmes and commercials as a child he went on to be further educated in the arts at the London Studio Centre, training under his current acting coach, Ian Dewer. Leaving the London Studio Centre in 1992, Nicholas returned to television work, including *Grange Hill*, *Happy Families*, *Peak Practice*, *The Bill*, *Casualty*, *London Bridge*, *No Nation*, *Second Sight* and several commercials. His first professional theatre job threw him in at the deep end with three parts in an outdoor performance of *As You Like It* (Stafford Gatehouse Theatre). Other theatre work includes *Dutchman* (Etcetera Theatre), a two-hander set on a New York subway, and *Clear Water* (Barbican Pit Theatre).

Nicholas recently appeared in *It's Not You It's Me*, a Bafta-nominated short film directed by Clara Glynn. He has also played Jason Hutton in the BBC daytime series *Doctors*. Nicholas has just finished a run of the play *Born Bad*, written by Debbie Tucker Green and directed by Kathy Burke at the Hampstead Theatre. Alongside his acting Nicholas has been working on his own scripts and film projects, setting up a production company, Big Smile Pictures, with Director Gary Wallis.

GABRIEL QUIGLEY
(Stewardess/Amy/Sarah)

Gabriel, who appeared at the Tron last year in Iain Heggie's *Love Freaks*, is a graduate of the University of Glasgow. She has had an extensive career on both screen and stage. Theatre credits include *Burning Bright* (V.amp Productions, The Tramway), *Top Girls* (The New Vic), *Mainstream* (Suspect Culture), *Outside Now* (Prada), *Dissent* (7:84), *Chic Nerds* and *15 Seconds* (Traverse Theatre Company), *Trainspotting* (tour), *Grimm Tales* (Leicester Haymarket), *The Gun* (Wildcat Theatre), and *Battle of Will* (Royal National Theatre Studio). Television appearances include *Still Game*, *Chewin' the Fat*, *The Karen Dunbar Show*, *Snoddy*, *Millport*, *Only an Excuse*, *Glasgow Kiss*, *Haywire*, *Life Support* and *Bumping the Odds* (all BBC); and *Taggart: For Their Sins* (STV). Film appearances include *Oathbound* (W.A.V.E. Productions), *Woof* (Dream On Productions) and *Man Dancing* (MD Films, directed by Norman Stone). On radio: *Penelope's Experiences in Scotland*, *Route Number 12*, *5 Men Went to Mow* and three series of *Millport* (all BBC Radio 4) and *Watson's Wind Up*, *Headcases* and *Dodgy Geezers* (BBC Radio Scotland).

MARISA ZANOTTI
(Co-Director)

Marisa Zanotti has been creating work in different media since 1987. Recent works include, *Shift/Shift Dreams* (video installation, Tramway), short films *Grockledance* and *Wipe Out*, Sony Play Station's Italian dub and *Butterfly* for Scottish Opera Steps Out. She created 8 full-length interdisciplinary works (1992–2000) with collaborators including sound artist Philip Jeck and designer Simon Vincenzi, through commissions from Tramway, New Moves International, Arnolfini and CCA. These toured internationally. She has consulted on staging and non-verbal communication for productions by the Traverse, Paines Plough, TAG, E.G.Y.T. and others.

As a performer she has worked with The Cholmondeleys (1989–92), Laurie Booth (1989), Wendy Houston (1992) and Stillben (1994). She is senior lecturer at University College Chichester . She is currently working on a film project *Gut-Maps*.

DAVID GREIG
(Writer/Co-Director)

David Greig was born and brought up in Edinburgh. He now lives in Fife. As a playwright his work includes the Fringe First winner *Stalinland*; *Europe*; *The Architect*; *The Cosmonaut's Last Message to the Woman He Once Loved in the Former Soviet Union*; *Danny 306+Me Forever*; *The Speculator* (winner of the Herald Archangel Award 1999); *Victoria*; *Dr Korczak's Example*; *Outlying Islands* (winner of Best New Play in 2003's inaugural Critics' Awards for Theatre in Scotland).

In 1990 he co-founded Suspect Culture with whom he has produced: *One Way Street*, *Airport*, *Timeless*, *Mainstream*, *Candide 2000*, *Casanova* and *Lament*. He has also translated Albert Camus' *Caligula* for the Donmar Warehouse and Laurent Gaude's *Battle of Will* for the National Theatre Studio.

Future projects include *8000M*, a show about high altitude mountaineering, for Suspect Culture.

SIMON VINCENZI

(Designer)

Simon has designed for theatre, performance, dance and opera in Britain and mainland Europe. Companies include Impact Theatre, Nottingham Playhouse, Anatomy, ENO, Royal Court, Scottish Opera and the Munich Biennale. He has been a regular collaborator with Rose English and was Head of Scenography at the Akademi for Figuretheater, Norway. His work as a director includes; *Heartless* (I.C.A.), *The Man with the Absurdly Large Penis* (Young Vic) and *The Dream Killers* (BAC). In 1994 he formed the company Bock & Vincenzi with the choreographer Frank Bock and has directed/designed *Three Forest Dances in a Room of Wood*, *Being Barely There I Saw You Too* and *Breathtaking*, a dance for three- to six-year-olds. Over the last four years Bock & Vincenzi have also been involved in a research period entitled *invisible dances*, collaborating with over forty artists around ideas of absence. This work will culminate in the Spring of 2004 with a large-scale show for theatre, a dance for the telephone, an installation, exhibition and publication.

CHAHINE YAVROYAN

(Lighting Designer)

Chahine's theatre work has included *The Cosmonaut's Last Message . . .* , for the Tron; *The Architect*, *The Speculator*, and *Outlying Islands* by David Grieg for the Traverse; as well as *15″ . . .* , *Iron*, *Gagarin Way*, *Anna Weiss*, *King of the Fields*, *Knives in Hens* and *Perfect Days*. He has also lit at the Royal Court, Manchester Royal Exchange, Hampstead Theatre, Nottingham Playhouse, ENO at the Lyceum, the Crucible, the Bush, the Young Vic, etc.

He has worked on dance pieces with Jasmin Vardimon, Yolande Snaith Theatredance, Rosemary Lee, Bock and Vincenzi, Anatomy Dance, etc., and on site-specific work with Station House Opera, *Dreamwork* at St Pancras Chambers, *Corridor* at Elizabeth Garret Anderson Hospital, the City of Bologna's New Year's Eve Celebrations, Coin St. Museum, *Push Parade* on The Cut, etc. He has also earned credits in the world of high fashion with Givenchy, Chalayan, Clemens-Ribeiro, Ghost, etc

Chahine is a longstanding People Show person.

GRAEME MILLER
(Sound Designer)

An artist, theatre-maker and composer, Graeme co-founded Impact Theatre Co-operative in 1978. His theatre works, which have a high physical and musical content, include *Dungeness, A Girl Skipping,* and *The Desire Paths.* With a mixed company of actors and dancers he produced the 1999 Place commission *Country Dance. Language Lesson* for Rosemary Lee's *One to One* series was also seen recently. He composes regularly for stage, TV and film and specialises in integrating sound design with musical composition.

His international geographical and sound-based works include *The Sound Observatory, Feet of Memory, Boots of Nottingham, Listening Ground, Lost Acres, Reconnaissance* and *Linked,* a public radio work with the Museum of London documenting houses demolished for an East London motorway. He is also doing preparatory work on new stage pieces.

Lost Sound (2000), a film with John Smith, documenting lost recording tape, toured internationally. A site-specific installation on the same theme, *Beside the A-Side,* opened Cornelia Parker and Jeff Macmillan's PEARL gallery in 2002 and was seen at Glasgow's New Territories Festival 2003. Meanwhile, his video installation, *Bassline,* opens at the Vienna Festival in 2004. Graeme is a Research Associate in Performing Arts at Middlesex University, and teaches Performance and Scenography.

Thanks to

MILLENNIUM HOTEL
GLASGOW

and

7:84 Theatre Company
Argos
Artistas Unidos (Lisbon)
Atalanta
Beer Paradise Ltd
Ross Connel
Cumbernauld Theatre
Lever Fabergé
Bob McMillan Signs
Katherine Mendelsohn
Mitchells Van Hire
Dearbhla Murphy
Royal Lyceum Theatre
RSAMD
Samsonite UK Livingston Branch
San Diego Convention & Visitors
  Bureau (www.sandiego.org)
Shorekarn Ltd
Roxana Silbert

Paul Sorley (Tramway)
Suspect Culture Theatre Company
TAG Theatre Company
The Traverse Theatre, Edinburgh
Visa International
wontdontwant.com

plus

Eric Barlow
Paul Blair
Steven Leach
Louise Ludgate
Alison Peebles
Marcia Rose
Jim Webster

and

the cast of the Artistas Unidos
workshops held in October 2002

tron

Tron Theatre Company

The Tron Theatre is Glasgow's leading small-middle scale producing theatre. Housed in a stunning collection of new and historic buildings, the Tron consists of a 230-seat auditorium and 75-seat studio, as well as bars and a restaurant.

The Tron Theatre Company produces four shows a year and also acts as an adventurous presenting house when not in production itself. Our work is mainly contemporary, text-based theatre and we strive to use the best Scottish talent available, alongside guest artists from the rest of the UK and abroad.

The Tron has an international reputation both as a producing and presenting company. In 2001 our production of Zinnie Harris's *Further than the Furthest Thing* toured South Africa, following performances at the Edinburgh Festival, the Tron and the National Theatre in London. The Company has also appeared in Canada and the US.

The Tron Theatre Company's most recent production was the first Scottish production of Patrick Marber's *Dealer's Choice*. Prior to that, the Tron produced *Shining Souls* by Chris Hannan, which enjoyed a sell-out success in February 2003 and recently won joint Best Production in the inaugural Critics' Awards for Theatre in Scotland. Other recent company productions include the Scottish premiere of John Mighton's award-winning play *Possible Worlds*, which also opened the inaugural Glasgow Six Stages Festival of Canadian theatre and dance; also, the premiere of Iain Heggie's *Love Freaks*, Martin McDonagh's *The Beauty Queen of Leenane* and the world premiere of *Further than the Furthest Thing* by Zinnie Harris, which received the Peggy Ramsay Award and was also the recipient of a Scotsman Fringe First and a Stage Award and an Evening Standard Award for Best Actress for Paola Dionisotti. From many notable past Tron Theatre Company productions, *Our Bad Magnet* (world premiere) by Douglas Maxwell, *The Cosmonaut's Last Message to the Woman He Once Loved in the Former Soviet Union* (Scottish premiere) by David Greig, *The Trick Is to Keep Breathing* (world premiere) by Janice Galloway and *Good* by CP Taylor feature among the highlights.

David Greig
San Diego

faber and faber

First published in 2003
by Faber and Faber Limited
3 Queen Square London WC1N 3AU
Published in the United States by Faber and Faber Inc.
an affiliate of Farrar, Straus and Giroux LLC, New York

Typeset by Country Setting, Kingsdown, Kent CT14 8ES
Printed in England by Mackays of Chatham plc, Chatham, Kent

The right of David Greig to be identified as author
of this work has been asserted in accordance with Section 77
of the Copyright, Designs and Patents Act 1988

'Band on the Run' by Paul and Linda McCartney
Lyrics reproduced by kind permission of MPL Communications Ltd

A CIP record for this book
is available from the British Library

ISBN 0-571-22194-7

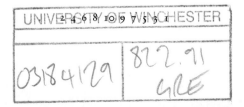

Characters

David Greig, the author
The Stewardess
The Pilot
Andrew
Marie
Daniel / Grey Lag, an illegal immigrant
The Woman, a telephone receptionist
Laura, a patient
The Counsellor
Pious, an illegal immigrant
Innocent, an illegal immigrant
Amy, a hooker
David, a patient
San Diego Cop 1
San Diego Cop 2
David A, someone who works in conceptual consultancy
David B, someone who works in conceptual consultancy
David C, someone who works in conceptual consultancy
Sarah, someone who works in conceptual consultancy
The Bedouin Tribesman
The Mother Superior
Patience / Amy, a real estate agent

Setting

The summer of the year 2000

Prologue

David Greig is sitting in an aeroplane seat.

David Greig It's the summer of 2000. I'm flying to San Diego, California. It will be the first time I have ever visited the American continent. I have been in transit for some eighteen hours now and for almost all that time I have been awake and drinking alcohol. When I left Scotland it was early morning and now, as I approach San Diego airport, it is early afternoon on the same day: June 10th 2000. On the plane I've been reading the *Blue Guide to San Diego*, and I've been particularly struck by two facts that it mentions. First: that San Diego has the highest quality of life of any city in the United States; and second: that despite being such a great place to live, San Diego has featured in almost no fictions, films, novels or plays, but it has, and I quote, 'served as the un-named backdrop for several episodes of *America's Missing Children*.'

I always like to know the facts about a place.

Here comes the Stewardess, she's called Amy.

The Stewardess passes and David stops her.

Excuse me, I couldn't possibly have another whisky by any chance?

Stewardess Of course, sir, one moment.

David I spent a ten-hour hiatus in Toronto Airport, drinking Molson in the tiny glass-fronted smoking lounge. During that period I watched a Filipino woman refuelling a 747, a tiny figure standing on the huge wing. The aeroplane tailfin had a picture of a greylag goose painted on it. Almost simultaneously I read in a two-day-old British newspaper about a Quebecois biologist who had heroically saved a flock of baby geese from extinction. The geese had been orphaned by some calamitous pollution event. Now the season was changing and the goslings were filled with an instinctive urge to migrate, but being motherless they didn't know where to go or what to do in order to satisfy their longing. The biologist knew that, at a certain stage in its development, the gosling's brain is a wet clay ready to imprint the image of its mother. He also knew that when a goose is at that stage, again I quote, 'any sufficiently large object which emits a rythmical sound' will become imprinted as the mother and the goslings will instinctively follow it. The heroic biologist stood before the lost goslings and made the calls of a mother until the geese learned to follow him. And then he got into a microlight aircraft and led the orphans, at the head of an elegant V, all the way to their summer breeding grounds in the Arctic. It has just, at this precise moment – 3.17 p.m. San Diego Time, 11.17 p.m. London time – occurred to me that *America's Missing Children* are perhaps drawn to San Diego because it is sufficiently large and emits a rhythmical sound.

The Stewardess brings David a whisky.

Thank you.

David drinks the whisky in one gulp.
A flock of geese, in a V-shape, rise from a marsh and fly north.
David rises from his seat.
The stage transforms.

Act One

ONE

David In the cockpit, the Pilot is preparing to land. The Pilot, Kevin, is very experienced. He'll soon be ready to retire, but right now he's at the top of his game. I'm not at all concerned about the landing. He has a voice that tells me he knows where he's going.

In the cockpit.

Pilot Ladies and gentlemen, good evening, this is your Captain speaking. You may have appreciated we have now started our descent into San Diego. If we don't get any air-traffic-control delays we should be landing in approximately twenty-five minutes from now, well ahead of schedule. If you haven't reset your watches from the time in the UK, it's a matter of winding back eight hours, weather in San Diego is fine, a very warm afternoon, 31 degrees Celsius, that's 82 degrees Fahrenheit. Thank you.

. . .

One to go

San Diego, Speedbird seven november level two-six-zero descending to level two-four-zero.

David Speedbird seven november, San Diego Centre roger, resume normal speed and maintain one-three thousand, two-five-zero knots, no holding. San Diego altimeter two-niner-eight-three.

A young couple, Andrew and Marie, are sitting in loungers by a pool.

This is Andrew, the Pilot's son, he's staying in a motel in the desert near San Diego. He's an actor in a film they're doing out there. This is his wife, Marie. They've got a kid, about nine months. Lovely kid, prone to allergies.

Marie Andrew.

Andrew Yes, love?

Marie Did you check on the boy?

Andrew Yeah.

Marie How was he?

Andrew Still asleep.

Marie How's he sleeping?

Andrew Soundly.

Marie How was his breathing?

Andrew It was regular, love.

Marie He wasn't on his front, was he?

Andrew No.

Marie No wheezing or anything?

Andrew No.

Marie I think the heat's giving him that rash.

Andrew Yeah.

Marie Did you have a look?

Andrew No.

Marie I don't think he's used to the water. Andrew?

Andrew Yeah.

Marie And did you touch his hand?

Andrew I did.

Marie Did he grasp your finger in his sleep?

Andrew Yeah.

Marie I worry about him.

Andrew You worry about him too much.

Marie I know.

Andrew He'll be fine.

Marie I know.

David Marie doesn't like the desert. She doesn't like it when Andrew's filming. She doesn't like staying in hotels. Marie would prefer to be at home, where she understands the hospitals.

Pilot San Diego approach, Speedbird seven november passing one-five thousand descending to one-four thousand and we have visual contact with Bravo.

David Speedbird seven november San Diego Approach Control expect runway two-six right.

Marie Have you got the baby monitor?

Andrew Yeah.

Marie Switch it on.

Andrew switches the monitor on. He passes it to Marie. The sound of a baby breathing close to a microphone.

David Speedbird seven november, turn to heading two-five-zero, join localiser for runway two-six right. Your traffic is twelve o' clock, five ahead now. Do you have the airport in sight?

Pilot We have the airport, but not the aircraft.

David Speedbird seven november, you're cleared the visual approach two-six right, reduce speed to one-six-zero.

Marie After every breath, I'm scared the next breath isn't coming.

Andrew It always comes.

Marie I know.

The breathing continues.
  Laura enters, wearing a hospital gown and carrying a mobile phone. She points the phone around, trying to get a signal.

David This is Laura, the Pilot's daughter. She's in hospital in London.
  She's not supposed to use that mobile, because it interferes with the kidney equipment in the urology ward.

Laura gets a signal and dials.
  In the cockpit a recorded voice counts down.
  The breathing continues.

Female Voice *Radio Altimeter.*

Marie Andrew – I know this is quite strange
  But I really want to pray.

Cockpit Alarm *Whoop, whoop, whoop, whoop.*

Andrew OK.
  I won't, if you don't mind, love, but you go ahead.

We hear the phone's ringing tone. The number Laura is calling is ringing.

Marie I have a feeling that I ought to.

Andrew On you go.

Marie Who shall I pray to?

Pilot Tower, speedbird seven november, heavy fully established two-six right.

Andrew Whoever's up there.

David Speedbird seven november San Diego tower, good afternoon, you're following a Boeing 767, caution wake turbulence, runway two-six right, you're cleared to land.

Marie Perhaps I ought to kneel.

Andrew It's probably all right if you just close your eyes.

Female Voice *Fifty above.*

Marie I ought to clear my head of any bad thoughts.

Female Voice *Decide.*

Marie And I should clear my heart of any bad feelings.

Pilot Land.

Andrew You'll be fine.

Female Voice 100 –

> *The phone continues to ring.*
> *The baby continues to breathe.*

Marie I should be utterly humble.

Female Voice 50 –

Marie What shall my prayer be?

Female Voice 20 –

Andrew You choose, love.

> *They pray*

Female Voice 10 –

Marie Dear . . . dear . . . whoever's up there –

Laura Please be there – please be in.

Marie Please look after us.

> *The shudderingly huge sound of a jet plane coming in to land.*

Marie looks up. Opens her eyes. She is almost
blown to the floor by the wind.
   The huge sound of the plane overwhelms her.
   A screech of wheels burning tarmac and the sound
of jets going into reverse thrust.
   Darkness.

Marie Andrew?

Andrew Yeah.

Marie There was definitely someone there.

TWO

Gloom.
   Laura, in her hospital gown, searching for a signal.
She finds it.
   She dials.
   A mobile phone ringing somewhere.
   The Pilot enters. He opens a huge venetian blind.
Behind the blind it is night. He switches a light on.
   The Pilot is wearing a vest, his shirt with epaulettes,
his tie, his hat, his Y-fronts and his socks.
   He scratches his arse.
   He looks around for the phone.
   He can't find it.
   It stops ringing.
   Laura exits.
   He looks at his watch.
   He sits down on the sofa and flicks through channels
on the TV.
   David is walking along dusty path beside a highway.
It is night, he is near a street lamp.
   Under the street lamp Daniel is standing. He has a
blue scar across his face and he is carrying a dead goose.

David I've been in San Diego for six hours and already I'm lost

The girl from the theatre who met me at the airport was called Amy, she gave me a car and a map. It was an automatic car, I set off on the freeway and I seemed to drive for hours just following everybody else. Then I was halfway to Mexico. I decided to stop and ask somebody.

Very, very slowly, David approaches Daniel. David proffers a scrap of a hand-drawn map.

Excuse me. I'm looking for La Jolla. I'm looking for the La Jolla Playhouse. It's a theatre. It's supposed to be near here

I wonder if you can help me.

Daniel takes the map. He looks at it.
   The Pilot picks up a copy of the San Diego white pages.
   He starts to flick through.
   He makes a call.

Pilot Hello, yes, is that The Palms?

Woman This is The Palms
   How can I help you?

Pilot I'd like a girl tonight, do you do – you do home visits?

Woman We do, sir, may I take you credit card details?

Pilot OK. The number is 7577 3543 1985 3776.

Woman Expiry?

Pilot 03/02.

Woman Thank you
   The girl's name is Amy, she's early twenties, very beautiful, very elegant, and she has a great sense of humour
   What name should Amy ask for, sir?

Pilot Kevin.

Woman And where are you, Kevin?

Pilot It's some kind of an apartment block
The complex is called Pacific View
And I'm Apartment 3, Block 2
OK?

Woman What address is that, Kevin?

Pilot Look, I don't actually know
I'm not from here. I'm –

Woman You're a visitor, Kevin.

Pilot Yes.

Woman Welcome to San Diego.

Pilot OK. Thank you.

Woman We'll have Amy with you in just about one hour.

Pilot Thank you.

Woman Thank you, Kevin. Goodbye.

David notices Daniel's feet. His shoes are torn, his feet bleeding.

David I recognise him. I know his face
It's unnerving
When I was in London, I was jostled in Camden
Market by someone with his face, the same torn shoes.
The same bleeding feet. The same blue scar
Who has a blue scar?

Daniel Is that your car?

David It's not my car, it's a hire car.

Daniel gives the map back to David.

Daniel What type of car is it?

David I don't know.

Daniel goes to investigate the car.

His name is Daniel
It turns out he was a fellow passenger on the plane to San Diego. He ran from the woods, under the fence, as the plane taxied slowly towards the runway
He grabbed the big wheels
He took one wheel, a friend called Edward took the other
He held on tight till the plane was in the air
Stomach in his mouth. Didn't fall
Then they were raised into the wings like chicks
Very cold in there
Eighteen hours of cold, thin air
He was strong, he never slept, never let go
Edward was dead when the plane landed
Daniel saw his friend's body tossed across the tarmac when the plane landed
But Daniel hung on tight. He had an appointment to keep in San Diego.

Daniel returns.

Do you mind me asking? Your scar, it's quite unusual
I've seen one like it before. Where are you from?

Daniel takes out a knife.
Daniel stabs David in the stomach.

You can't stab me
You can't.

Daniel kneels beside David. He kisses him lightly on the cheek.

Daniel I'm sorry.

David I know.

Daniel I'm sorry.

David That was the wrong thing to do, Daniel
That was a big mistake. Believe me
Daniel
Don't go
Don't go.

Daniel picks up the knife and runs.
David lies in the dust.
The Pilot is standing by the window, flicking
through the channels, looking out of the window.
He checks his watch.
The phone rings.
He picks it up.

Pilot Yes?

Woman The girl's having difficulty finding you, Kevin
Can you be a little more specific about the address,
please?

Pilot I'm sorry, I don't know the city
It's called Pacific View.

Woman Can you see the Pacific there?

Pilot No
At least, I don't know
I can see the Hilton Hotel
The top of the Hilton Hotel
And, when I look out of the window, there's a freeway
And it intersects with another freeway
It's a complex, a complex of apartments.

Woman OK, Kevin. I'll tell the girl. We'll try to get her to
you.

Pilot OK.

David Hello? Hello? Is anybody there. Hello?

Laura enters and sits down in front of the Counsellor.

Counsellor Hello, Laura. Sit down
How are you today?
Mmm?

A very, very long silence.

Can you say anything about how you feel today?

The phone rings again.
The Pilot picks it up.

Pilot Yeah.

Woman Hello, Mr Kevin?

Pilot Just Kevin.

Woman Kevin, Amy called me just now and she says she's been along the freeway up and down two times now, past the Hilton, and she says she can't find any apartment called Pacific View.

Pilot OK. OK. Right.

Woman We need some more detail of the address here? Can you find out the actual address?

Pilot OK. Wait
I'll go outside and I'll see if I can see any street names, or any numbers or anything
Can you hold
For two minutes?

Woman I can hold.

The Pilot puts his trousers on quickly and leaves.
The Counsellor pours some water from a jug into a paper cup and offers it to Laura. She takes it. She drinks it.

Counsellor You seem very low today, Laura.

A very long silence.
   Laura is not hostile.
   She looks at the Counsellor.

What can we do to help you, Laura?
   What can we do to help you today?

A long pause.
   The Counsellor pushes a box of tissues towards
Laura.
   Laura pushes the tissues back.
   The Pilot re-enters the apartment.
   The phone is still off the hook.

Pilot Hello? Are you still there?

Woman Is that you, Kevin?

Pilot Yeah. Look, I went out and had a scout around and the street seems to be called Coronado Boulevard. That's the name of the road which is running in front of the apartment here.

Woman Coronado Boulevard.

Pilot OK, and there's an intersection and I don't know what the other street is called but I suppose if you look at the map and you see Coronado Boulevard and you go along it until you're in the vicinity of the Hilton, then you should be able to see if there's a complex of apartments or something marked on the map.

Woman OK, Kevin. Don't worry.

Pilot Do you have a map in front of you?

Woman I don't have a map, Kevin, but don't worry, Amy has a map. I'll relay this information to her.

Pilot Where is Amy just now?

Woman She says she's just by the Hilton.

Pilot Well, look, you know I can see the Hilton from here so she must be very nearby.

Woman Don't worry, Kevin. We'll find you. OK, I'll call you once I've talked with Amy. OK.

Pilot OK. Bye.

The Pilot puts the phone down.

Counsellor It's better if you can talk, Laura. If you can say something. Anything. It just . . . it can help us to start trying to . . . help you get better.

Laura opens her mouth.

. . .

Laura I.

Counsellor . . .
    Yes.

Laura Don't.

Counsellor You don't.

Laura . . .

Counsellor Yes?

Laura . . .

Laura looks at the Counsellor, pleading.

Counsellor It's OK.

Laura leaves the consulting room.
    The phone rings again.

Pilot Hello.

Woman Kevin?

Pilot Yes. Hello.

Woman Kevin, I have got to tell you that Amy is looking at her map and she says there is no such place as Pacific View.

Pilot But I'm here. I'm staying here.

Woman But Kevin, you can't see the Pacific.

Pilot No. Not from this apartment.

Woman So why is it called Pacific View, Kevin?

Pilot I don't know. How should I know?

Woman Kevin, my concern here is, that you are some kind of crank
  Some kind of English crank caller
  Can you allay my fears on that?

Pilot As a matter of fact I'm Scottish and I gave you my credit card. I'll pay Amy for the time she's been looking.

Woman Well, Kevin. I'm not sure . . .

Pilot Look, I'll walk to the Hilton. Tell Amy to wait in the Hilton car park. I'll walk to the Hilton and I'll find her there.

Woman OK, Kevin, that sounds like a good idea. I'll relay that to Amy.

Pilot Thank you
  Tell her I'll be . . . what, ten minutes.

Woman Bye, Kevin.

The Pilot leaves the apartment.
  Marie enters, she sits on the sofa, she switches on the television.

Marie Love . . .
  Love? Come through . . .

Andrew enters.

Andrew What is it?

Marie *America's Missing Children*'s on TV.

> *Marie sits down. They watch.*
> *The Pilot walks down the dusty path beside the freeway.*

David Excuse me . . . excuse me . . .

> *The Pilot sees David.*
> *He goes towards him. Kneels.*

Pilot Oh my God
Jesus
Are you OK? You're hurt? You're bleeding? Can you hear me?

David I can hear you.

> *Darkness.*

THREE

Laura is sitting on the sofa, watching television, wearing a hospital nightgown. She is clipping her nails.
Under the freeway, beside a small muddy gutter.
Daniel is hunkered down a distance away beside a small cooking stove.
Pious and Innocent are sitting on cardboard sheets. In front of them is a melon, the bloody knife, a guide to San Diego, some string, and a zippo lighter.
Pious is holding a small notebook and a stub of a pencil.

Pious One melon
One penknife
One book
One quantity of twine
One cigarette lighter.

Innocent OK.

Pious OK.

Innocent So – in the event of my death . . . in the unhappy event of my death . . .

Pious Really it's just a matter of who gets what.

Innocent OK
In the event of my death . . .
And the funeral arrangements.

Pious And the funeral arrangements.

Innocent OK
In the event of my death
I don't like to think about it.

Pious You have to think about it.

Innocent I don't like to think about it
I may have to – but I don't have to like it.

Pious The sooner you decide who you're going to leave it all to the sooner you can stop thinking about it.

Innocent You just want the melon.

Pious I want nothing.

Innocent You've had your eye on it all week.

Pious I don't want it.

Innocent You want to have sexual intercourse with my melon.

Pious I don't want the melon.

Innocent Then you won't get the melon.

Pious It's entirely your decision.

Innocent OK.

Pious In the event of my death, I, Innocent – which is you – hereby will that my estate be passed over to . . .

Innocent Oh . . . It's a bit much, all this.

Pious Usually, what we do, is we say that we will leave everything to our wives. In your case, you have no wife.

Innocent I don't need a wife. I have a perfectly good melon.

Pious You never know, you may find a wife – so can I put that your estate passes to your wife, and then – if you have no wife – that it passes to any children you may have.

Innocent Wives, children. I slave away all my life. For what? For what? I tell you, Pious, it certainly puts things in perspective.

Pious However, in the event of the deceased having neither wife nor surviving issue – to whom does the estate pass?

Innocent You're so transparent
You just want it to be you.

Pious As a matter of fact I don't.

Innocent 'As a matter of fact.' Do you have a will?

Pious Yes.

Innocent Who do you leave everything to?

Pious I have left it to you.

Innocent Really?

Pious Really.

Innocent Really?

Pious In trust.

Innocent What does that mean?

Pious It means you have to look after it, until the boy is
twenty-one
    Then you have to give it to him.

Innocent That's what I'll do then. That sounds just fine.

Pious OK.

Innocent Except the knife.

Pious You don't want the boy to get the knife?

Innocent No
    The knife will only get him into trouble
    I want the knife to go to . . .

Pious I'll look after it, if you like, until he's twenty-one.

Innocent Don't ever give him the knife.

Pious Never?

Innocent The poor creature's terrified
    He's barely out of the forest. You can't go handing him
knives.

    A pause.

Pious Innocent . . .

Innocent Yes.

Pious I lent the boy the knife
    I sent him off to kill a dog.

Innocent You didn't ask me.

Pious You weren't here.

Innocent You're a sly one.

Pious I'm sorry. I didn't know you had such strong
opinions about it.

Innocent You're a cunning jackal.

Pious It was a genuine mistake.

Innocent First the melon, now the knife – what's next – the string?

Pious I'm sorry.

Innocent Did he kill a dog?

Pious He killed a bird
A lovely fat goose.

Innocent Well, don't do it again
The boy's got a head full of electricity.

Pious He doesn't know the ropes, that's all.

Innocent We have to look after him
Is that in the will – custody of the boy?

Pious If you die, I will look after him
If I die, you will look after him
Promise?

Innocent Promise.

Pious Poor lad.

Innocent We'll just have to hope you die first.

Pious What about the knife?

Innocent In the event of my death
Use it to carve my name in a piece of wood
Then I want everyone to sing my favourite song.

Pious What's that?

Innocent 'Band on the Run.'

Pious For goodness' sake.

Innocent That's what I want

And then put the knife in a parcel and post it to whoever is the President of Nigeria with a note telling him to use it to kill himself.

Pious OK.

Laura stands, she takes off her hospital nightgown, she stands in her pants. She feels the fatter parts of her body with the calm of a butcher. She chooses her buttock. She uses the nail clippers to snip a chunk out of her buttock. She winces in pain. She holds the small chunk of flesh up to the light. She walks over to the cooking pot, she puts the chunk of flesh in the pot.
A pause.
She dips her hand in the boiling water and removes the tiny chunk of flesh.
She eats it.
She chews carefully, then swallows.
She faints.
Darkness.

FOUR

An apartment in San Diego.
The apartment phone is ringing.
The Pilot enters, carrying David.

Pilot We'll get you to hospital, son, don't worry
You're going to be OK.

David I'm not worried
I'm fine.

The Pilot puts David on the sofa and answers the phone.

Pilot Yes? Oh
Yes, this is Kevin

Look, I'm really sorry – something came up
Yeah
No, please . . . I am terribly sorry
There was an emergency here
I know
Look. Please, will you convey to the girl, yes, to Amy,
will you convey to Amy my sincerest apologies
. . .
Well – I really don't know what else to say
. . .
Yes. Yes I realise. Next time I will try to be more
specific about the address. I really am sorry
. . .
I apologise for the inconvenience
. . .
Goodbye.

David You've missed an appointment.

Pilot Yeah.

David I'm sorry.

Pilot It wasn't important.

The Pilot is dialling 911.

David We'll have to get that sorted out.

Pilot Yes
Hello, could I have an ambulance, please?
Yes, it's for . . .
Oh Christ, look I don't know
It's called Pacific View Apartments
No. I can't be more specific
Do you know where we are?

David We're in San Diego.

Pilot Look never mind
I'll . . . we'll get a taxi.

He puts the phone down.

Let's get you bandaged up or something.

The Pilot leaves. He comes back with a T-shirt, he tears the T-shirt into strips.

What's your name?

David David.

Pilot I'm Kevin.

David You're a pilot.

Pilot I am – that's right.

The Pilot starts to bandage David with the strips of T-shirt.

David You fly the new Boeing 777.

Pilot I do. How did you know that?

David I worked it out
Today was British Airways inaugural flight to San Diego in the new extended-range 777s. You're English.

Pilot I'm actually Scottish.

David I didn't know you were Scottish. You don't have the accent.

Pilot You're interested in planes, are you?

David I certainly am.

Pilot I used to be as well.

David You're not any more?

Pilot Well, no, of course I am.

David You still believe in them though.

Pilot Yes.

David Oh, that's good

. . .

You know the tail-fin designs for British Airways – the mad paintings?

Pilot Yeah?

David Do you like those?

Pilot I hate them.

David Me too.

Pilot Things change. It's a new world
I don't understand it
Now, don't you worry, David
We'll go out on the street and we'll find a taxi and we'll get you to hospital.

David I'm not worried. It's going to be fine
You seem to know what you're doing.

They leave.
Laura, in her hospital gown, is standing by a payphone.
She dials a number which she has written on a scrap of paper.
Somewhere in the apartment a mobile phone rings.
Eventually the phone stops ringing.

Pilot (*voice on the phone*) Please leave a message after the beep.

Laura . . .
Where are you?

She puts the phone down.
She limps off.
The Pilot holding David on the dusty path beside the highway.
David is visibly ill now.

The Pilot is frantically trying to flag down a car.
None are stopping.

Pilot Stop. Stop. Please stop . . .

David What time is it?

Pilot It's five o clock in the morning, David.

David I feel very tired
I've been awake all night.

Pilot You just stay awake
We'll soon have you all kitted out
Don't you worry.

David I'm not worried
I'm just tired.

Pilot Why don't they stop? STOP STOP PLEASE.

David They're on their way to LA
They work in LA, which is an hour's drive from here
They can't stop or they'd be late for work.

Pilot You just . . . that's the ticket. Stay standing
Just stay standing.

David I think I'll just have a sleep
Just for ten minutes
I can't keep my eyes open.

Pilot You just stay awake there
You just stay awake
C'mon
Talk to me
Talk to me.

David I won't die
I'm just tired.

Pilot Stay awake. Tell me about – tell me about San Diego
C'mon

I'm new here
WAIT STOP STOP FUCK
FUCK YOU FUCKING JESUS.

David Don't swear
Please don't start swearing.

Pilot I'm sorry, I'm sorry. Jesus
Look – c'mon.

Holding David up, the Pilot finds the Blue Guide *in his pocket. He thrusts it into David's hands.*

Tell me about San Diego
Where's good places to go?

David Well, San Diego, you may be interested to know that San Diego has the highest quality of life in the whole of the United States.

Pilot Really?

David Yes
San Diego is also unique in having its airport so close to the city centre.

Pilot I noticed that.

David is reading the guide.

David The approach to San Diego at night is one of the most beautiful approaches of any airport. Because you see the ocean on one side, the vastness of the Pacific Ocean, and then on the other side you see the elegant glass towers of the downtown area. And the lights of the Coronado Bridge. Which stretches across the bay.

Pilot Tell me more.

David I'm really quite tired.

Pilot Tell me more. Tell me more.

David Well, San Diego was built mostly in this last century, and mostly since 1950. It has an exact reproduction of Shakespeare's Globe theatre in Balboa Park and it also boasts a zoo with a worldwide reputation.

Pilot Perhaps I'll take a trip down there.

David It's certainly worth an afternoon.

Pilot STOP. STOP. STOP.

David In 1986 San Diego was the setting for the film *Top Gun* starring Tom Cruise and Kelly McGillis. San Diego, while not having many films actually set here, is often used as a substitute for other American cities because it is a very convenient place in which to film . . .

David falls.

Pilot Get up. C'mon, son. Get up.

David I can't do that.

Pilot Talk to me.

David I'm not dying, I just feel a little nauseous.

Laura enters with a kitchen knife.
She takes off her hospital gown.
She examines her body.
Innocent is plucking the goose, talking to Daniel.
Pious is sharpening the knife.

Pious Where do you come from, boy?

Daniel I come from Jos.

Pious Jos. Named after Jesus our Saviour. City of Tin
I know Jos. It's lovely place. Very temperate
Is there still a swimming pool at the Plateau Hotel?

Daniel There's a pool. But there's no water.

Innocent Who is your father, boy?

Daniel My father's dead.

Innocent I will be your father
Pious will be your mother
. . .
What is your name, boy?

Daniel My family call me 'little shit'.

Innocent Hmm.

Pious He needs a better name than 'little shit'.

Innocent Son, you killed a fat goose today
For us to eat at this, the feast of your naming
A meaty white goose to eat
Since you brought us the gift of a goose, we'll call you
Grey Lag
After the goose.

Grey Lag Grey Lag.

Innocent Are you a Christian, a Muslim, or a pagan?

Grey Lag I don't know.

Innocent Do you believe in God?

Grey Lag Yes.

Innocent Then let us pray – Holy Father, help us push the desert back tomorrow morning
Help us shape the meat into patties tomorrow afternoon
Help us to answer the telephone tomorrow evening
Dear Lord, thank you for the goose
Thank you for bringing young Grey Lag here to us
Roger
Over and out
Please cut into the flesh

Laura cuts a thin slice from her body.
She has to hold herself back from screaming in pain.

The sound of a car screeching to a halt a little way up
the road.
The Pilot runs towards the car.

Pilot Please. Please. Wait.

Amy walks along the dusty path by the side of the
road to where David is lying.

Amy Oh my God.

Pilot We have to get him to hospital.

Amy Oh my God, oh honey.

She kneels by David and holds him.
Laura starts to bandage herself up.

Pilot Will you drive us?

Amy Who did this to you, honey? Can you hear me?

David Hello.

Amy Who did this to you?

David I don't really know.

Amy Here, call 911. Get them to send paramedics. It'll
be quicker
Tell them we're on Coronado Boulevard
Just by the Pacific Heights.

She gives a mobile phone to the Pilot.

Oh honey . . . you hang in there for me, honey.

David Miss.

Amy Yes, honey.

David Are you a hooker?

Amy What kind of question is that?

David I've never met a hooker before
Outside of a work context
Not to talk to.

Amy Well . . . good.

Pilot Yes – hello, this is an emergency, a young boy, he's been stabbed. Coronado Boulevard just by Pacific Heights, please hurry. It's absolutely vital . . . please. OK.

David What's it really like? Being a hooker?

Pilot They say ten minutes.

Amy Shit, gimme that phone, mister.

She takes the phone.

Get down here now, for Christsakes, the kid's delirious.

The Pilot kneels by David.

Pilot How're you doing, son?

David She's a hooker.

Pilot Yes, son.

David Wow.

Pilot You were telling me about San Diego
Tell me more.

David I think I like San Diego. I feel very drawn to it
San Diego is surprisingly familiar
I recognised it as soon as I stepped off the plane.

Pilot It seems like a fairly anonymous sort of place to me.

David Yes
Not special at all
The sort of place one moves to, for a job

And you know what, no trip to San Diego is complete without a swim in the Pacific. The temperature of the ocean at this time of year is 72 degrees.

Pilot It sounds wonderful.

David When you bathe in the ocean at San Diego – the water is exactly the same temperature as blood
We could go later today if you like?

Pilot That's a good idea.

David I could take you and the hooker to the beach.

Pilot Yeah.

David Miss? Would you like to come to the beach with the Pilot and me?

Amy Sure, honey.

David We'll go in the afternoon.

Pilot Yes.

David I'm actually slightly frightened.

Pilot Yes.

David I think I'm dying.

Pilot Yes.

David I think that's what's happening.

> *Laura puts the meat into a frying pan on the fire.*
> *Laura faints again.*
> *The flashing red lights of the paramedics.*
> *The Pilot lifts David, cradled in his arms.*
> *He walks towards the lights.*
> *Amy is still kneeling.*
> *David is dead.*
> *Marie is weeping.*

Marie That was very sad.

Andrew Yeah.

Marie That's what it's like out there.

Andrew You shouldn't watch these things, love.

Marie Andrew.

Andrew Yes, love.

Marie I want to pray again
  Will you pray with me?

Andrew No, love
  But you pray. You go ahead.

  Darkness.

  End of Act One.

Act Two

ONE

The Nevada Desert.
Andrew, dressed as a pilot, is talking to the Pilot, who is also dressed as a pilot.
They sit at a small table and are drinking bottled beer.

Andrew I'm on a routine flight – to the Gulf – when suddenly the cockpit door bursts open and this guy comes in – balaclava over his face – gun – tells me not to panic. Tell's me, 'Stay very, very calm.' I say, 'OK.' He says, 'Right. Are you calm?' I say, 'I'm calm.' He says, 'Right.' I say, 'Wait a minute. Is anybody hurt out there?' He says, 'Not yet. Not yet, but we'll shoot the fucking stewardess if you try any funny business with the fucking plane. Anything the slightest fucking bit funny we'll shoot her. In fact,' says the man, 'if you do anything, if this plane does anything that we don't understand – and we don't understand much about aeroplanes – so if this plane starts doing something and we don't know exactly why it's doing that thing, we'll panic and we'll kill the stewardess. Is that clear?' I say, 'It's clear.' Now, we know each other already from the time in the airport where I find out who's on my flight and my eyes go a bit misty when I hear her name. She's called Amy. Well – what with that moment and the moment when I'm walking on to the plane and I pass her in the aisle and I say, 'Hello Amy,' and she says, 'Ray . . . it's been a long time,' and I say, 'Yeah,' and she says – I don't know, some other shit – so we know that there's a bit of a thing between me and Amy. So anyway, the hijacker says, 'Take the fucking plane to fucking Baghdad.' I start plotting the course. Suddenly, the plane starts emitting this . . . rhythmical sound. 'Thump, thump, thump.' Like great wings beating . . . The hijackers say, 'What's that?' And I say, 'I don't know,' and then the hijacker says, 'Shoot the stewardess.' The co-pilot tries to overpower them and he gets shot, and I cradle him in my arms, the poor fucker – but the shot's damaged the fucking something or other and we're going down and the there's people being sucked out of the plane and then kaboom – we're crashed in the middle of the fucking sand. After that, it's a kind of Moses thing, as I shepherd the survivors through the desert to Abu Dhabi. Amy survives – and in the desert we fall in love.

Pilot Sounds good.

Andrew But is it true?

Pilot I don't know.

Andrew Is it plausible
  Take it apart
  You're a pilot, Dad, you know.

Pilot Most pilots would attempt to co-operate with the hijackers.

Andrew OK.

Pilot Try to get to know them.

Andrew Sure –

Pilot Try to stay calm.

Andrew Yeah and . . . so is it – the story – does it ring true?

Pilot I don't watch films, really. I don't know
  It's a highly unlikely combination of events
  How's Marie?

Andrew Fine.

Pilot And the boy?

Andrew Terrible allergy thing, but he's great, he's really great.

Pilot I hope you're looking after Marie?

Andrew That's not what we do nowadays.

Pilot What do you do nowadays?

Andrew I don't know exactly. We're a sort of team.

Pilot Just make sure you look after her.

Andrew . . .

Pilot Have you spoken to your mother?

Andrew She's OK.

Pilot Good.

Andrew You spoken to her?

Pilot I – it's – no.

Andrew What about you?

Pilot Me?

Andrew You all right?

Pilot Yes. Bit tired. Hard night. That's all.

Woman Andrew, you're needed on set
  It's the desert decision scene.

Andrew OK.

Pilot They need you.

Andrew C'mon, you can watch the scene
  I make a decision in this scene
  It's a good scene.

Pilot I'd better go, really.

Andrew No, c'mon, stay – we'll have a drink after.

Pilot I'm a bit tired.

Andrew Stay in my trailer. I've got a great trailer
Have a sleep. Relax. Chill out
Then we'll have a drink.

Pilot OK.

Andrew You sure you don't want to watch?

Pilot Yeah. Thanks. But . . . I'm a bit tired.

Andrew Sure. OK. We'll – we'll have a drink after, then.

Pilot After.

Andrew exits, the Pilot sits.
Pious, Innocent and Grey Lag enter. Pious is holding
three shovels.

Pious Take a shovel.

Innocent Give him the black shovel.

Pious I was already going to.

Innocent The black shovel is the one I started with.

Pious It's just a shovel.

Innocent It was my shovel. Now it's yours.

Pious OK. What we do is, we dig sand from this side and
we move it over to this side.

Innocent Like so.

Pious That's it. Only don't go so fast. If you go too fast
you'll be tired out.

Innocent Don't listen to him. He's a lawyer. He's not
used to manual labour.

Pious We move the sand back across to the other side
of the highway.

41

Grey Lag The sand will blow back in the night.

Innocent Of course.

Pious The sand blows back in the night. And then in the morning we shovel it to the other side again.

Grey Lag I didn't come to San Diego to shovel sand.

Innocent Son – you don't mind me calling you son?

Grey Lag I don't mind.

Innocent Son, if we didn't shovel the sand it would very quickly take over the city.

Pious Three days, they've calculated.

Innocent In three days the city would be covered in sand.

Pious The desert is hungry for this city.

Innocent If you want to make money from the meat and the telephone calls then you'd better start shovelling sand. Because the sand gets in the meat, and it gets in the wires.

Grey Lag . . . I didn't come to San Diego to shovel sand.

> *Grey Lag throws down the spade and walks off.*
> *Andrew enters, crawling. He crawls for some moments. He stops.*
> *He slumps.*
> *Innocent and Pious start shovelling sand.*

Innocent It's just a phase.

Pious You're putting too much pressure on him.

Innocent He has to learn.

Pious He's very sensitive.

> *A Stewardess enters crawling.*
> *She crawls up to Andrew.*

Stewardess We have to rest. The old lady can't go any further.

Andrew If we don't make the city we're all gonna die.

Stewardess She's gotta rest.

Andrew Shit. Shit. Shit. Goddam. Goddam.

Stewardess What are we going to do, Ray? If we go on, the old lady's gonna die. But if we stay here, we're all gonna die.

Andrew Where is the old lady now?

Stewardess She's over there. She's sleeping.

Andrew takes out a knife.

Oh Ray, no.

Andrew Amy, it's the kindest way.

Andrew crawls back towards the old woman. The Stewardess falls weeping to the earth.

Stewardess You bastard God! God you goddam son of a bitch!

Laura enters.
  She is limping and bandaged, and wearing her hospital gown.
  The Counsellor sits, beckons her to sit down.

Counsellor Good morning, Laura.

Laura Morning.

Counsellor How are you feeling?

Laura OK.

Counsellor Good.

Laura . . .

Counsellor . . .

Laura . . .

Counsellor You've been cutting yourself, Laura.

Laura Yes.

The Stewardess gets up, brushes herself down. She looks out into the lights, squinting.

Stewardess How was that?

Voice Fine
Thank you.

The Stewardess brushes herself down.
   Andrew walks on.

Andrew D'you fancy a drink?

Stewardess Sure.

Andrew My dad's here. He's a real pilot. Come and have a drink.

They walk off.
   Pious and Innocent are shovelling sand.
   Grey Lag enters.
   They carry on shovelling sand.
   Pretending not to notice.
   Grey Lag sits, watches.

Counsellor Why are you cutting yourself, Laura?

Laura I'm not cutting myself exactly.

Counsellor What then?

Laura I'm butchering myself.

Counsellor You're certainly doing yourself harm.

Laura At least I'm eating.

Counsellor . . .

Laura I do cook the meat first. In fact I want to be cured.

Counsellor Well, that's good, Laura, that's a start.

Laura In salt. Or maybe smoked.

Darkness.

TWO

The Pilot sits at a table in the desert under an umbrella.
The Stewardess and Andrew are looking at him.
They are drinking from a bottle of whisky.
The Pilot is sitting in silent abjection.

Stewardess Andy, listen. I think your dad needs you to hold him right now.

Andrew You do?

Stewardess Yes I do
I really think he needs you to hold him.

Andrew Right

  . . .

Stewardess You go, Andy. You go hold your father.

Andrew goes over. He kneels beside the Pilot. He can't
quite find a position which means he can hold him.
The Pilot continues to cry. The Stewardess watches
from a distance. Andrew slowly reaches out his hand.
He touches the Pilot's hand. The Pilot squeezes
Andrew's hand.
    The Stewardess watches.
    Pious and Innocent enter dressed in a uniform of
red dungarees and red baseball caps. They start to
clean the surface of the metal table.

45

Grey Lag enters dragging a large, heavy see-through polythene bag full of mince.

Pious Are you watching?

Grey Lag Yes.

Pious You scoop the meat up with your hand like so.

He scoops out a handful of mince.

You slap it down on the table.

He slaps it down on the table.

Then you form it into a pattie . . .
Like this.

He forms it into a pattie.

Then you place it here, to form a pile of patties.

He places it a little in front of him.

When you have a tall pile of patties, you take them to the freezer
You understand?

Innocent He has that look again.

Pious You can do it.

Grey Lag What is the meat?

Innocent Pig meat.

Grey Lag Which parts of the pig?

Innocent All of it.

Grey Lag Even the eyes?

Innocent Yes, eyes, nose, lips, all of it.

Grey Lag I didn't come to San Diego to shape pig lips into patties.

Innocent I knew it.

Pious Don't get angry.

Innocent He didn't come to San Diego to . . . Bloody hell.

Pious Innocent. He's only a boy.

Grey Lag I didn't come to San Diego to handle pig noses.

Innocent Listen to me, you little shit
You're not in Jos now
If we don't shape the meat into patties the Americans will not eat the meat. And the meat will fill up the storehouse
And it will rot. And it will liquefy. And this liquid meat will run in the gutters of San Diego, it will soak into the sand and turn it into sludge, it will penetrate the telephone exchanges and cause them to explode in a shower of blood. Do I make myself clear?

Grey Lag picks up a handful of meat.

Good.

Grey Lag throws the meat onto the floor.
Grey Lag walks away.

Pious We have to be patient with him.

Innocent I know.

Pious You called him a little shit.

Innocent Did I? Oh, I did. Oh damn.

Pious You should apologise to him.

Innocent Oh, I feel terrible.

Innocent goes to leave.

Pious Wait. Wait till he comes back. He'll come back when he's calmed down.

They go back to forming patties. Sadly. Serious.
The Pilot stands up. He walks away.

Pilot I've got to go. I've got to get back to the airport.

Andrew It was nice to see you, Dad.

Pilot Good to see you too, son.

Andrew Yeah.

Pilot Look after yourself.

Andrew Will do.

Pilot Nice to meet you, Amy.

Stewardess You too, Kevin.

The Pilot exits.

Andrew Shit.

Stewardess What's wrong?

Andrew All my life he's a fucking cunt
All my life he's a fucking stone
All my life he's a fucking stone carved into a cunt
shape
And now he's weeping
Wet
What the fuck am I supposed to say?

Andrew exits.
The Stewardess follows him.
*Laura enters, limping, wearing a hospital gown. She
sits on the sofa and switches the television on. It is a
cookery programme.*
*David enters. Also wearing a hospital gown. He sits
down beside her. She moves up a little.*
Grey Lag comes back.
He stands watching Pious and Innocent.

Innocent Listen, son, I'm sorry
   I called you a little shit earlier on
   I really shouldn't have done that
   I had no right
   I just want you to know that I'm sorry.

Pious We don't think you're a little shit all.

Innocent Not at all.

Pious But sometimes you behave in a way which makes us feel like saying the words 'little shit'. D'you see?

Innocent No, Pious, it's more specific than that
   When you say that you didn't come to San Diego to form pig lips into patties
   I can't stop myself from calling you a little shit
   It's the tone of voice you have
   That's what it is.

Pious But the important thing is, we don't think you are one
   That thing.

Innocent No.

Pious You're a wonderful young man.

Innocent And we love you.

Pious So, you just hunker down. We'll do these patties. And afterwards we'll go to the call centre together.

Innocent Here . . . wait.

   He reaches into his pocket and brings out the length of twine.

You can play with this if you like.

   He gives him the twine.
      Grey Lag hunkers down.
      He plays with the twine.

49

Laura You're new.

David New. Yeah. Only just come.

Laura What you in for?

David Chronic attention deficit disorder.

Laura What?

David What?

Laura What's chronic attention deficit disorder?

David I don't know
I can't concentrate long enough to find out
. . .
No, that's a joke. That's a joke
Really I'm in for Tourette's.

Laura Right.

David Fuck!

Laura What?

David No, it's a joke. It's a joke.

Laura You're an irritating little runt, aren't you?

David I know. I really am. I'm really sorry. Really.

Laura What you in for then?

David Sex addiction. No, it's a joke. It's a joke.

Laura I'll fucking stab you.

David No, really. It's attention deficit disorder. Really it is.

Laura What's that then when it's at home?

David I'm not interested in anything. It really pisses people off.

Laura Fair enough.

David What about you?

Laura Suicidal. Manic. Self-harmer.

David What's that all about, then?

Laura Very low self-esteem mostly.

David Why's that?

Laura Well, they think it's for some other reason
But as far as I can tell
It's because I'm a useless piece of shit.

David You're very pretty.

Laura You interested?

David I am.

Laura Really.

David Too late. I'm bored again
It's a joke. It's a joke.

Laura I can see why you piss people off.

David Yeah.

Laura You got any fags?

David Yeah.

Laura Gi's one.

David Here.

He gives her a fag. She lights it.

Laura You hungry?

Darkness.

THREE

The ringing of many phones.
    Andrew is sitting on the sofa watching television.
Marie is curled up on the sofa with her head on his knee.

Marie Andrew.

Andrew Yeah.

Marie You know I love you.

Andrew Yeah.

Marie And you know I'd never do anything to hurt you.

Andrew Yeah.

Marie You or the boy.

Andrew Yeah.

Marie Well the thing is . . .
    The thing is . . .
    No I can't say it.

Andrew OK.

There is a metal bed. With paper across it. Beside the
bed is a bedside table. On the bedside table is a box of
Kleenex. And some pornographic magazines.
    The Pilot enters.

Pilot I'm here to see Amy. I called?

Woman Certainly, sir. You're Kevin, aren't you?

Pilot Yeah.

Woman That's right. Eight o'clock. Kevin
    My name is Amy, nice to meet you. I'm Amy's assistant.
If you'd just like to wait here for a moment, sir, make
yourself comfortable, she'll be with you in just a moment.

The woman leaves.
Kevin sits on the bed.
He looks at the pornographic magazines.
Pious, Innocent and Grey Lag enter. They sit down
on three swivel chairs and they put telephone headsets
on.

Innocent OK. When you answer the call you say – 'Good morning, Pacific Heights, Amy speaking, how can I help you?'

Pious OK. In San Diego everybody is called Amy.

Innocent And then let them speak, until they seem to have stopped whatever it is that they want to say. And then you say: 'May I have your account number, please?'

Pious Whatever they say after that, you repeat it back to them, until they stop.

Innocent And then you say, 'May I have your date of birth, please?'

Pious And then you do the same thing. Just repeat what they say.

Innocent And your mother's maiden name.

Pious And then you say it back to them, and then you pause, and then you say – 'I have a cousin called –' whatever it is they said.

Innocent Then you let them say another thing.

Pious And then you say, 'Isn't that amazing?'

Innocent And then you say, 'Thank you for calling Pacific Heights'
And when they have emptied themselves of all that they want to say
The call is ended and you begin again.

Pious Do you want to try? You try.

Pious reaches over and clicks a remote so that Grey Lag's headset is connected. The phone stops ringing. They cast encouraging glances at the boy. As if to say – 'Go on . . . go on.'

Grey Lag . . .

   . . .

   . . .

   . . .

   . . .

   . . .

I didn't come to San Diego to answer telephones.

Pious reaches out quickly and grabs the headset off him.

Pious For goodness' sake, you little shit.

Innocent Pious.

Pious I've had it up to here with you
I've had it.

Innocent Calm down.

Pious attempts to hit the boy. Innocent holds him back.

Pious I could show you the back of my hand, son.

Innocent Calm down. Calm down.

Pious You have no idea. No idea
If we don't answer these phone calls then the Americans will just store up their thoughts until their heads are full and then one day it'll all come pouring out in a great torrent of gibberish and they'll talk and talk and talk until they deflate like balloons
And then they'll lie exhausted on the streets with the meat piling up in warehouses and the desert lapping at their ankles

You have no idea
You arrogant – self-centred –

Grey Lag walks away.

The cheek of the boy.

Innocent We just have to be patient.

Pious I know. I know.

Innocent He's new to all this.

Pious I know.

Innocent The thing is, when he's at his most unpleasant
That's when he most needs our love.

Pious You're right. You're right as always.

Innocent C'mon
Let's get to work.

Pious Good morning, Pacific Heights, Amy speaking,
how can I help you?

Pious and Innocent answer phones.
Amy enters.
The Pilot looks at her.
She walks towards him and sits on the bed next to him.
They look at each other.

Pilot I – sorry – just thought I'd . . .

Amy I know.

Pilot I don't want to.

Amy Of course not.

Pilot I would like to have saved him.

Amy Me too.

They hold each other's hand.

Marie It's just the thing is . . .
I think I've started to believe in God.

A pause.

Andrew God?

Marie Yes, love.

Andrew Right.

Marie God, love, really believe.

Andrew OK.

Marie Andrew.

Andrew Yes, love?

Marie It's quite a big thing.

Andrew I can imagine.

Marie I really feel it.

Andrew Good.

Marie Really feel it. It's wonderful.

Andrew That's great, babes.

Marie I think
I think I found something.

Andrew What?

Marie We've brought a boy into a terrible world
So terrible even his skin reacts to it
And I've never known what to do about it. How to
cope.

Andrew Yeah.

Marie I just wander round being scared all the time.

Andrew Sure.

Marie But I think I've found the answer.

Andrew Yeah?

Marie I'm going to become a nun.

Andrew What?

Marie A nun, love. A nun
I think I need to pray more.

Andrew Oh, for Christ's sake.

Marie Don't be like that.

Andrew Don't be like that! Don't be like that! A nun? Don't be like that! A nun? A nun?

Marie You'll wake the boy.

Andrew A nun?

Marie Andrew
I – I – just . . . I just . . . I'm sorry
God
I thought
Jesus
Andrew. I thought you would . . .
God
OK. Forget it. Forget it
I won't be a nun
Forget I said anything
Just forget the nun thing
I should never have mentioned it.

She leaves.

Andrew Where are you going?

Marie I'm going to bed.

Andrew Wait. Wait . . . love . . .

He follows her.

David and Laura enter. They go up to the fridge.
Laura takes a polythene bag out of the fridge. She puts
it on a plate. She opens up the bag and takes out about
four slivers of meat, different cuts.

David What you gonna do with it?

Laura Roll them in flour and egg
Make rissoles.

She takes a bag of flour and an egg and she gives them
to David. She takes the plate of meat.
    They exit.
    The Pilot and Amy on the bed.

Pilot I'd better go
I've got to fly a plane to London.

Amy Yeah.

Pilot Listen. Thank you.

Amy I know. Me too.

Pilot If you're ever in London or . . .

Amy If you come back – gimme a call.

Pilot Yeah.

Amy You know what?

Pilot What?

Amy If you come back –

Pilot Yeah.

Amy I wanna take you to the beach
Like the kid said
Let's say go to the beach and say goodnight to the kid.
The Pilot leaves.
Darkness.

FOUR

*Under the bridge, Pious, Innocent by the light of a
cooking fire.*
  *Grey Lag is kicking the melon about in the dark,
playing football with it.*
  *David is lying on the bed, looking at the pornographic
magazines, using a small torch to help him see.*
  He looks at them really fast.
  Flicking through them.

Pious I'm tired.

Innocent Me too.

Pious Long day.

Innocent Long day.

Pious It's always harder when you've got kids, isn't it?

Innocent Yes
  Good though.

Pious Yes
  Good.

Innocent Look at him with that melon
  He loves that melon.

Pious He's good
  He's a good player.

Innocent You think so?

Pious Potential future international
  He could play for the Super Eagles, that boy.

Innocent You might be right.

Pious I'm telling you.

Innocent He's got the temperament.

Pious And he's strong.

Innocent Perhaps we should write to the manager
See if we can get a trial for him.

Pious Good idea.

Innocent We'll do it tomorrow.

Pious Yeah
There's something I want to ask him
Hey, hey, Grey Lag!

Grey Lag What?

Pious Come here. Come here.

Grey Lag picks up the melon and approaches them.

Grey Lag What is it?

Pious There's something I wanted to ask you.

Grey Lag What?

Pious Well, you don't have to answer if you don't want
to
But . . .
Why did you come to San Diego?

*Grey Lag reaches into his pocket. He takes out a
postcard. He gives it to Pious.*

Innocent A postcard of San Diego.

Pious I've never seen one of these before
It looks beautiful
Who gave it to you?

Grey Lag My mother sent it
To me
It is adressed to me
See

The name at the top
That's my name.

Innocent I can't read the writing.

Pious Give it to me.

Pious peers at the writing and tries to decipher it.
Laura enters carrying a plate.

Laura You wanking?

David No. Bored. Can't concentrate.

Laura takes the magazines and puts them in the
bedside cabinet.
She sits beside him on the bed, holding the plate.

Laura I made these for you.

David They smell great
What's in them?

Laura Got some herbs from the garden
Apart from that it's just me.

David Can I have one?

Laura If you want.

David looks at the rissoles.
He eats one.
She watches him eat.

Pious Dear Daniel, As you may know, I am singing
backing vocals in a band called Wings on a world tour
of America. Tonight I am in San Diego. The tour is going
very well and I love singing. I think of you all the time
and I know I'll see you soon. I'm so proud of you
    You must know so many things that I can only dream
of
    All my love
    Mum.

Innocent Wings – your mother sang backing vocals in Wings?

Pious Daniel.

Innocent My God.

Pious Daniel.

Daniel When I was a very tiny baby. My mother was cradling me in her arms as she attended to a chewing gum stall. In Lagos
She used to sing to me. And she had a very beautiful singing voice. One day, she was singing to me when a man came up to buy chewing gum from her. And he listened to her singing
And he said he was making a record right there in Lagos
And he asked her to sing on his record. So, right there and then she put me on her back and went to sing. But I was a bad child. And I cried in the recording studio. And so my mother had to give me to her sister to look after. And when she got married to a man who lived in Ibadan she gave me to her sister, who became ill with fever and gave me to her sister who lived in Jos and that is where I lived until one day I took a mammy wagon up to Kano. And when I got to Kano I found the airport and a man showed me how to catch the wheels of planes as they take off. So I did that until I found a plane to take me to San Diego.

Pious It must have been very cold.

Daniel Very cold
Very cold.

Laura How does it taste?

David Crap
No, it's a joke, it's a joke.

Laura Don't.

David It tastes fucking beautiful, Laura
Tastes fucking great.

Laura Eat another.

David does.

Innocent How old are you, boy?

Daniel I'm twenty-six.

Innocent No way.

Daniel I am.

Pious We'll help you find her.

Daniel picks up the melon and takes it off to kick the ball about again.

Laura You can eat them all if you want.

David Can I?

Laura I really want you to.

He eats the other two rissoles.

Innocent McCartney came to Lagos in 1974
The boy is too young
This card is from someone else, to someone else
He just found it.

Pious He says he's twenty-seven.

Innocent No way.

Pious Maybe there is another band called Wings.

Innocent Most likely whatever mother he had was stuffed full of heroin and flown to Amsterdam.

Pious You think so?

Innocent Don't you?

Pious I think we should try to find her.

Innocent Tomorrow.

Pious Tomorrow.

They take out their blankets.

Laura You're smiling.

David Sorry.

Laura Don't be sorry.

David I'm all full up.

Laura I want to kiss you.

David Do you?

Laura Yeah, I do.

David Well, you bloody can't
No, joke. Joke
Do you really?

Laura Really.

David God. I dunno.

Laura Lie on the bed.

David lies on the bed.
   She climbs up.
   Kneels astride him.
   He tries to sit up.
   She pushes him down.

Laura You're skinny. You need feeding up.

Two San Diego policemen with guns come in.
   They pull the guns on Pious and Innocent. Grey
Lag hides in the darkness.

Cop 1 Police. Don't move.

Cop 2 Hands in the air.

Pious and Innocent put their hands in the air.

Cop 1 Get down.

Cop 2 Hands on your heads.

Cop 1 Stay down.

Pious and Innocent lie down with their hands on their heads.
The two cops search them.
Laura leans down to David and kisses his lips.
She leans back.

Laura Bored yet?

David No.

The cops find the knife on Innocent.

Cop 1 Who's the knife?

Innocent It's my knife.

Pious It's my knife, I lent it to him.

Innocent It's my knife.

Cop 1 shows the knife to the other Cop.

Cop 1 Is that the knife?

Cop 2 Sure looks like the knife.

Cop 1 Who's knife is this?

Innocent It's my knife.

Cop 1 OK. Get up.

Innocent gets up.
The Cop leans down and picks up a stone.
He throws the stone.

Go get the stone.

Innocent looks at them.

Get the fucking stone.

Innocent turns.
He walks slowly towards the distant stone.

Laura leans down to kiss David again. Lingering.
The Cop shoots Innocent in the back.
He falls.

Laura Bite my lip.

David bites her lip.

Oww.

David Sorry.

Laura It's all right
Full of iron
Builds your bones.

Darkness.

End of Act Two.

Act Three

Darkness.

In the darkness, music: 'Band on The Run', Wings, at the instrumental break.

A sudden burst of flame.

Innocent's body lies on a pyre in flames.

Daniel and Pious stand before it. On the ground in the dust, the melon, cigarette lighter, the string and the knife.

The music is coming from a tinny flatbed tape recorder playing an old cassette.

Laura is lying in a hospital bed.

David is sitting on the bed, wearing his hospital gown. They are holding hands.

Darkness.

ONE

The Pilot, in uniform, his hat on his knee, sitting on the hospital bed.

Grey daylight through a large window.

Laura standing in front of the window in her hospital gown, bandaged, looking out.

An area with coloured bean-bags, a low table and a laptop.

Laura turns to the Pilot. Silence.

Laura Can I wear your hat, Dad?

Pilot If you like.

She approaches him and takes the hat.
She puts it on.

67

Laura It's warm. From your head
  Do I look like I know where I'm going?

Pilot Of course.

Laura That's what a hat does for you.

  She turns and looks out of the window.
  David A, David B, David C, and Sarah enter. They
  are dressed casually, with an impeccable grasp of the
  contemporary. David A approaches a laptop, which
  he sits beside and casually types into.
  David A, David B and Sarah sit around on the
  bean-bags.
  The words capitalised in brackets are typed by
  David A on the laptop screen.

David A C'mon
  C'mon
  We're onto something
  OK
  Let's push this
  Let's talk about the village. (VILLAGE) What does a
village have? David?

David B Villagers.

David A Villagers – people – people who live in the
village
  David, yeah?

Sarah The villagers are possessed of a sense of belonging.

David A A sense of belonging. Belonging. (BELONGING)

Sarah Is there something about birth – place of birth –
Do you have to be born in the village?

David C Born 'into' the village.

David B Brought up in it.

Sarah Because isn't there a symbolic entry moment? A ritual of . . .

David B A ritual of initiation of circumcision.

David A Surely not.

Sarah No – yes – A symbol of entitlement. A visible symbol
Which is like –
Yes. Sorry but yes
Tribal markings.

David B Sorry can I –

Sarah Go ahead.

David B It isn't tribal markings.

Sarah OK.

David B It's your name.

Sarah It's your name.

David A Your name. (NAME) That's good
Oh that's good.

Sarah There's a dream I have.

David A Dreams. Give me dreams. Dreams work.

Sarah A picture that appears in my dreams
. . . No, it's gone.

David C Sorry, just while I've got this – fire.

David B Yes. Fire. Fuck. How could we forget fire?

David C A place of fire.

David B Yeah, but also a place of intoxication. A place of drinking or . . . smoking . . .
A transformative place.

Sarah A pub
Whoop-de-do, boys
The village has a pub.

David A (PLACE OF FIRE) Great. Great.

David C Wait. Wait. It's not a pub it's a – public space
Sorry.

David B Go on.

David C I'm thinking of the village square
I'm thinking of the long afternoons
The sun's high so the men sit in the shade . . .

David B Under the banyan tree.

Sarah Like it. Tree. So . . . tree symbol.

David A A banyan is a tree?

David C This was in Nigeria, I saw this in Nigeria.

David A (BANYAN)

Sarah A tree, but it's also a symbolic centre.

David A More
Dave?

David B I don't know. Pass.

David C Men chew betel nut
They spit juice on the ground
In a lazy arc
It's slow. It's a rhythm.

Sarah Wait – the picture. I've got the picture.

David A OK.

Sarah OK, so it comes from a dream.

David A OK.

Sarah But it's very clear.

David A OK. Describe it, Sarah, let's see the picture.

Sarah OK. There's a well.
And women. Women are . . . They must be going to the well to fetch water. It's hot, so the air is shimmering
I can hear a sound, there's a low sound. A rhythmic sound.

David This is good. Push it.

Sarah A sound
It's not even words
It's . . . um a um a um a . . . you know . . . It's not even in a language maybe
And
This is the sound that's coming from the women
In this picture from this dream
In the dream I have a sister
Which is weird
And she's teaching me . . . the movements . . . um a um a . . .

David B Can I just –

Sarah No, I'm going to finish this –

David B Sorry.

Sarah I have a sister and – the thing is I feel an overwhelming sense of . . . It's as though this sound is a prayer
Of thanksgiving
For the going on of things.

David A Hmm.

David B It isn't a place. It's a sound.

Sarah OK. But . . . what I'm saying is . . . in this picture maybe there is a place . . .

David B A crèche?

Sarah It's not a crèche.

David C Is it a well?

Sarah I don't think –

David B Praying.

David C Is it about water, the gathering in of water?

David B A place of praying – to – to who?

David A Yes. Yes. Take it on. This is good.

David B Um.

David A Dave?

David B A place at the centre of it all
A hut
Sarah's sound
A hut in the doorway of the hut . . .
The shaman
The magician.

Sarah The chief.

David A Bingo. (CHIEF)

Sarah Smoke. Darkness. A place you're not allowed into.

David B Not so much a hut.

David C Not so much a hut as a chamber?

Sarah A secret chamber?

David B The people witness their chief turn to enter the chamber.

Sarah It's dark. It's behind a door. And it contains . . . everything.

David A And it is the cockpit.

David B *and* **David C** God, yeah.

David A (THE PILOT IS THE CHIEF)
The Pilot is the chief.

Sarah Yes. Yes. He wears the crown.

David B He wears the crown.

David A OK. Good. Good. Let's look at the plane now
Let's look at the plane.

*David brings out a large model of an aeroplane and he
takes off the roof of it to reveal the seating. They start
to take the model apart.*

Laura I tried calling you.

Pilot I know.

Laura Why didn't you call back?

Pilot I didn't get the message until – I was already flying
here anyway
I knew I was going to see you.

Laura Sorry.

Pilot I'm sorry. I should've let you know.

Laura No I'm sorry.

Pilot How . . .
How are you?

Laura . . .

Pilot The nurses said you were . . .

Laura Cutting myself. Yeah.

Pilot Laura . . .

He tries to touch her gently.

Laura Get off.

Pilot I'm sorry.

Laura No. I'm sorry.

Pilot I wish I could –

Laura Yeah. So do I.

Pilot Understand, even.

Laura Me too.

Pilot You know I . . .

Laura Yeah.

Pilot And your mother . . .

Laura I know. It's fucking hideous
    Last night, I saw the geese fly over
    Means it's summer, doesn't it?
    Must be going north I suppose
    Great big beautiful V
    Mad. Fucking insane. How do they know? I don't
know.

Pilot It's in the brain.

Laura In the brain
    Goose-brain radar or something
    D'you know?

Pilot Nobody knows
    Some people think they can read the stars
    Some people think they can read geography
    Nobody knows.

Laura Geese do
    Know where they're going
    Don't even know that they know
    But they do.

Pilot Yeah.

Laura Remember we saw them
   A mad flock by the sea
   And they all took off
   Fucking all took off in a mad explosion.

Pilot When was this?

Laura Don't you remember?

Pilot Oh. Yeah. I think so.

Laura And you pointed at boss goose
   The goose in front
   And you said: 'That's what I do Laura
   I fly. That's Daddy's job.'

Pilot God. Yeah.

Laura I wanted to go with them
   Wherever it is they're going
   I want to run and jump through that window and
follow the fuckers all the way to wherever.

Pilot Greenland, probably.

Laura Fucking Greenland
   Must be fucking . . .
   . . .
   . . .
   . . .
   . . .
   Have your hat back.

   Pilot takes back his hat.

Pilot Don't, Laura.

Laura What?

Pilot Don't . . . please don't . . . the window . . .

Laura What? Oh . . .
   Oh God

Sorry
Yeah
Scrape me up off the car park and all that
Sorry.

Pilot Please don't
Promise.

Laura Yeah. Yeah.

Pilot They'll help you here
They'll help you out of it.

Laura Dad
I wish.

Pilot They can, Laura. Drugs nowadays.

Laura Yeah, drugs.

Pilot It will. Trust me. It will go away
You weren't always like this
You were cheerful. You were a cheerful kid.

Laura Yeah. Before I fucked up.

Pilot Before . . . before . . . what?

Laura I dunno
I fell down a big well.

Pilot . . .

Laura . . .

Pilot If I ever did anything wrong, Laura
If I ever – your mother and I . . . if I we ever . . .
Was it the divorce? D'you think? Was it that? That
sent you like this?

Laura No. I don't think so.

Pilot Then what? Tell me, please.

Laura I honestly don't know
   I . . . It . . .
   It feels like I'm hungry all the time.

Pilot Are you eating?

Laura Not hungry. Like I'm hungry.

   She slumps.

I want to go home.

Pilot I'll take you home.

   She hugs him, desperately. He tries to respond. Unsure of what's required.

I'll take you home
   I'll take you home
   You can stay in the flat, in Surrey . . . with me.

Laura No.

Pilot In Hong Kong then, with your mother.

Laura No.

Pilot Anstruther, the cottage in Fife, the seaside.

Laura No.

Pilot The *gite*. The *gite* in Provence.

Laura No.

Pilot Tell me, Laura. Anywhere. I'll buy you a house. Anywhere
   Anywhere you'll be happy.

   She breaks away from him.

Laura I'm fine, Dad
   I'm sorry
   I'll stay here
   They'll help me get over it.

Laura sits on the bed.
　*David puts a moving image of a flying aeroplane on
the computer.*
　He stands before it.

David　A person needs to know where they are, where
they're going and what time it is
　But when people fly they feel like they've lost these
moorings. They feel anxious
　And this anxiety acts as a disincentive to air travel
　Nobody wants to feel anxious. We want to feel safe,
on earth
　But in reality – time and place no longer exist in the
world
　There is no time in the city
　There is no place on the high street
　The safety of the ground is an illusion
　Co-ordinated universal time – aeroplane time – is the
only time we experience which never changes
　The cabin of the aircraft is the only space where we
can be certain that we belong – we have a ticket with our
name on it
　On the seat in front of us there is a map which shows
us clearly where we are going
　And we are going forwards
　Did you know, the average child born in this century
will spend more of their lifetime on an aircraft than they
will with their grandparents? That is fact.

Laura lies down on the bed.

The human mind evolved to cope with a community of
two hundred and fifty-six people – which happens to
be the number of passengers carried by the Boeing 777,
two hundred series.

Laura curls up on the bed.

We don't know how planes work

We don't want to know how planes work
We want to believe
We want to be part of the rhythm
We want to belong
We want to see familiar things
Ladies and gentlemen
. . .
The aircraft is your village
'Welcome home.'

Laura starts sucking her thumb.
   The Pilot kisses Laura, he covers her up as though putting her to bed. He exits.

TWO

Marie, in a nun's habit, is kneeling and praying silently.
   Pious and Daniel on a patch of dusty ground with Innocent's possessions.
   There is also a pile of ashes in front of them: Innocent.
   Daniel is using the knife to carve 'Innocent' into a wooden block.
   Laura curled up on the hospital bed.
   David enters. He sits on the bed.
   She doesn't move.

David I'm hungry.

Andrew enters.

Andrew Love? You've been praying all night, love
Come to bed
   . . .
Love, you have to eat
You have to sleep
You have to . . .
   . . .
Come on, love.

Laura How do you want me?

David In me.

Laura Tell.

David I want to feel full up again
Like before.

Laura Do you want me tender?

David Yeah.

Laura Do you want me wrapped in foil and butter
And baked
Slowly, slowly, so all my juices keep their flavour.

David Sounds good, yeah.

Andrew D'you mind if I put the telly on?

Laura Or do you want me flash-fried over a hot flame
Hissing and spitting
Herbs rubbed into my skin, rare and red on the inside.

David God yeah.

Andrew I'll put the telly on.

Andrew puts the telly on. Sits on a bean-bag. Watches.

Laura Or d'you want me marinaded in wine
Paper-thin strips of me
Soaked in delicious booze.

David Bloody hell.

Laura Or stewed with chilli
So I burn your mouth off.

David Fuck
I just want what you want.

Laura I want you to eat me raw.

David God. You sure?

Laura You scared to?

David No.

Laura Go on then.

David Just take a bite?

Laura Taste first
Lick first.

David . . .

Laura Go on.

David gets into bed with Laura. He crawls between her legs.

Andrew The whole nun thing
The whole – you being one – does it utterly preclude sex? I mean
There's the praying
And so on
But – does it utterly utterly demand that you don't have sex at all? Is that a stipulation? I only ask
I only ask because. Love
We haven't . . .
And . . .
Babes, I know there's a hell of a lot of sadness in the world
Jesus, you don't need to tell me about it. I'm carrying a ton of it on my shoulders. But babes. Seriously. I don't think God would mind . . .
Would he
Could he mind? If we . . . expressed our . . .
He made us sexual beings after all
We have to conjoin, in union, blessed union, isn't it? And we conjoin . . . in a holy way, and . . .
That's a form of worship isn't it?

It's a form of prayer in a way
Isn't it?
When two people lose themselves in each other's
bodies it's sacred
Isn't it?
I think, in fact, I know that God, if and when he
makes himself available to you in revelation, I know that
he, if you asked him would make it very plain to you by
sign or symbol that he wanted you to make love
With me
Now
. . .
Besides, love
You do look fantastic in that habit.

Laura screams.
  Marie falls sideways. In a faint.
  Andrew approaches her.
  David emerges from the bed.
  He swallows something.
  Laura kisses him.
  They hold each other.

Pious We should scatter his ashes.

Daniel Two times now.

Pious He wanted me to look after you.

Daniel Two times.

Pious I'm going to look after you now.

Daniel Twice. I've scattered my fathers' ashes.

Pious We'll have to be a team.

Daniel Two fathers.

Pious We'll have to look after each other
  We'll have to help each other

He's watching us
He's in heaven watching us and . . .
Daniel.

Pious is overtaken by grief.
  He holds on to Daniel.
  He shakes.
  He breaks off and regains his dignity.

Daniel Tell me, Mother, in San Diego: do they suppose that we are ants? That there are so many of us? Do they suppose that we are dogs? That we love them? Do they suppose that we are cattle? That they can eat our bodies?

Pious You mustn't be angry, son.

Daniel Do they suppose that I came here to shovel their sand?

Pious God will see to it.

Daniel When I was a boy in Jos
  I lived nearby a white family
  I walked into their garden one day
  A boy, about my age
  He was playing with a chemistry set
  I went to see what he was doing
  He threw blue acid in my face
  I ran home
  And my mother's sister's sister's sister held me
  And I asked her
  Did the white boy maybe suppose that I was a thief?
And she said, 'No, you little shit. The white boy supposed that you had come to kill him.'

Pious Everything is written in a map in God's head.

Daniel I know. I know what's written.

Pious We can't know.

Daniel I know. I know exactly where I'm going. I know exactly
　It's in a map in my head.

Pious Son. You're grieving.

Daniel I didn't come to San Diego to bury my father.

Pious Son
　You came to San Diego to find your mother.

Marie is on the couch.
　Andrew is caressing her face.
　She wakes up.

Andrew Did you see God?

Marie No.

Andrew Maybe it was just a passing thing and now he's gone.

Marie No
　He'll come back.

Pious Everyone needs a mother and a father
　You lost you father, son, and you need a real mother
　Not some bloody old man
　Not some stupid old lawyer
　Not me. A proper mother
　We'll find your mother, son
　Your mother is in San Diego
　And we'll find her
　We're a bloody team.

Darkness.

THREE

Desert.
Andrew, in the costume of a pilot, is crawling across the desert, near the point of death.
Some distance behind him crawls the Stewardess.
Pious and Daniel sit, beside them a handwritten sign that says: 'Are you my mother?'
The Counsellor is sitting.
Laura comes in, limping badly, wearing her hospital gown.
She sits.

Counsellor How are you today, Laura?

Laura Great.

Counsellor That's good.

Laura Feel fucking fabulous.

Counsellor . . .

Laura No, really
Really I do.

Counsellor I believe you.

Laura No you don't.

Counsellor I believe you.

Laura It's written all over your face
I'm happy.

Counsellor I believe that some of your symptoms are in remission.

Laura Yeah.

Counsellor Why do you think that is?

Laura It's because I'm in love.

Counsellor Love?

Laura Love? Don't you fucking add a question mark to that word, you cunt.

Counsellor There's a hostility in what you're saying, Laura
    You are aware of that?

Laura I'm happy. I'm in love. I feel like I'm fucking walking on air.

Counsellor That's great.

Laura You don't seem to think so.

Counsellor Laura
    Love can be . . .
    It can be . . . it can take . . .
    Innappropriate forms.

Laura What?

Counsellor It can be – a – love is – itself – it can be – a disturbance – a . . .

Laura I don't believe this.

Counsellor There is appropriate love
    And there is . . . for example . . . masochistic love
    And whilst there is a mild masochism in almost all relationships
    It is not appropriate, Laura, for your lover to eat your flesh
    . . .
    . . .
    We found the rissoles.

Laura Love
    It's bloody love.

Counsellor How do you know if it's not . . . an infatuation . . . a . . . dependency . . .

Laura It is
It's a crush. I fancy him. It's lust. It's dependency. It's masochistic. It's pathetic. It's delusional. It's all-encompassing
It's obviously just a chemical reaction in my brain
He looks like my father. He talks like my brother.
He's the part of myself I have still to come to terms with. I want him to eat me. I want to eat him. I want him in a way that I can't possibly begin to describe to you except possibly by performing 'Love Me Tender' at an Elvis karaoke night
I feel like I've suddenly fallen into the arms of an old, old city. Rome. He's Rome and I'm a Roman
Love
No question mark.

Counsellor Your dad came to see you yesterday?

Laura I don't want to talk about my dad
I want to talk about David.

Counsellor How did you feel? Talking with your dad?

Laura Like a useless piece of shit.

Daniel This isn't going to work.

Pious Patience
Patience.

Laura has exited.
David is now sitting opposite the Counsellor.
David is bored and distracted.

Counsellor How are you today, David?

David Mm?

Counsellor David.

David Sorry.

Counsellor How are you today?

David There's a smell
There's a smell. Did you fart?
Oh no. It's my fingers.

Counsellor How are you finding things?

David Looking. Usually looking
In drawers
Try and remember where I put them.

Counsellor I mean how are you . . .

David Joke. Joke. Seriously? Seriously? Being absolutely serious? To answer the question
Just taking it seriously
To give you – speaking honestly – being frank. Full and frank. The bottom line? The truth, the whole truth and nothing but?

Counsellor Yes.

David I suppose . . .
What was the question?
No, joke. Joke
I ate a bit of Laura
Can you believe that? I can't believe that? I ate a bit of a girl.

Counsellor I know.

David Fuck me.

Counsellor Which bit, David?

David Can't tell you
Secret
Tasted nice, I can tell you that
I love her

I'm finally living. Know what I mean
There's a point
Can you believe it
Jesus
Love – mad – fucking bananas – Jesus – love – me –
girl – There's a point
What time is it?

Counsellor It's midday.

David There's something on telly
It's been nice
Cheers
Honestly. I feel much better after that. I really do
Thanks. Sincerely. Honestly
Load off my mind.

Counsellor We're going to move you to a different ward,
David.

David Are you?

Counsellor We thought a change of scene . . .
It might . . . help you.

David I refuse.

Counsellor David . . .

David No. Seriously. Joke. Joke
Good idea
Like your talk
Change is as good as a rest
Can I go now?

Counsellor David – you can choose what you want to do
Nobody's keeping you here
But you have to start thinking about your choices
You have to start thinking ahead
You have to reflect on what your choices force us to do
to you.

David is very unsure about whether to go or whether to stay.

Daniel My mother is not in San Diego
She lied.

Pious We'll talk to Mr McCartney
We'll speak to his people
We'll find your mother.

Pious and Daniel leave.
      A Bedouin tribeseman in a white dishdash is holding a water carrier in the middle of the desert. Andrew stops at his feet. He looks up. His mouth open.
      The Bedouin kneels and pours water into Andrew's mouth. Andrew drinks thirstily. Then he slumps.
The Bedouin walks towards the Stewardess. He pours water into her mouth. She too drinks thirstily. She too slumps.
      The Bedouin tribesman starts calling orders to other tribesmen.

Bedouin Hamdi. Bring the camels
Put the woman on my camel and the man on yours
We can walk beside them
We'll take them to the village
We'll give them clean water from the well
The woman can stay in the women's compound – with the aunts and the grandmothers
They'll tend her
The man can come to my tent
We'll give him water and dates and wash his feet
Then we will hold a feast for these guests
Then, when they are fully recovered
We'll take them to Abu Dhabi.

Voice (*from off*) Cut. Thank you. Thank you.

David leaves.

FOUR

In a bar. The Pilot is drinking a pint of Guinness, Sarah is drinking gin.
    In a bar. The Bedouin is sitting with an empty bottle of beer.
    Marie praying.
    Laura, in her hospital gown, with a knife, in front of the window.
    A woman sitting at a desk with a telephone.

Sarah As you know, the airline's looking at a complete redesign concept to bring us into the twenty-first century. As part of that process we're looking at a few quite small changes to the pilot's role in the whole airline experience. I just want you to look at some ideas.

Pilot OK.

Sarah You've got to criticise – OK? Really lay into them. Any flaws – expose them
    That's the idea of the excercise.

Pilot Well, I'll . . . certainly try.

Sarah Good. Don't hold back.

Pilot I won't. Look, before we start
    Would you like another drink?

Sarah Yeah. I'll take another gin. Gin and bottled tonic, please. Double.

    The Pilot goes to get the drinks.
        Sarah gets out her Palm Pilot.
        Pious and Daniel enter. They look out of the window.

Pious Look, son. This window is so high that we are in the jetstream

Look at the city. The desert. The sea
Paradise. San Diego is most beautiful place on the
whole of the earth.

Daniel It doesn't belong to us.

Pious walks up to the woman at the desk.

Pious Miss. We want to make an appointment to see
Mr Paul McCartney.

Woman No.

Pious It's very important.

Woman I don't care.

Pious We have to find out about the recording of 'Band
on the Run'.

Woman Go away.

Pious We'll wait.

Woman You can wait as long as you like
Paul McCartney's never going to see you.

Pious We will wait.

David enters.

David We've got to run.

Laura They're going to take you away from me.

David No way. I won't let them. We're going to run.

Laura It's pointless.

David No. No, there's a point.

Laura What is it?

David You. And Me. Now. It's . . .

Laura Where?

David Scotland. The goose place. By the sea.

Laura How?

David I've made a plan.

Laura What?

David We wait till it's dark
Then . . . then . . . we sneak downstairs. OK?

Laura OK.

David Then we wait till the guy at reception's looking the other way.

Laura OK
Then what?

David I dunno. I got bored after that.

Laura I love you.

David No, seriously. We run like fuck.

They kiss.

C'mon. Get proper clothes on.

The both start to get dressed, intermittently kissing and caressing each other as though they are each the other's oxygen and they must get regular draughts to live.
Andrew enters with two bottles of beer. He sits down with the Bedouin.

Andrew There you go. They didn't have any Guinness, I'm afraid.

Bedouin What is it?

Andrew Singha. Thai. Great stuff.

Bedouin I'm very fond of Guinness. When I was a student, I used to go down Kilburn High Road and drink Guinness with the Irish

Brilliant. Lovely people. Always happy to see a Palestinian

The Palestinians are the Irish of the Middle East: this guy – Flynn, great guy – big big drinker – he used to say that

Happy days

Cheers

Hows the wife?

Andrew Christ. Don't start me.

Bedouin It's like that, is it?

Andrew There's a whole nun thing happening with her at the moment

It's driving me mental.

The Pilot comes back.

Pilot Gin.

Sarah Thanks

OK . . . right

There you go: it's all on there.

The Pilot squints to read the Palm Pilot.

Andrew Since we had the kid, she's had this thing about the suffering in the world. You know? And . . . well, one night she decided to pray and she had a vision of God as an aeroplane. And she said that she was imbued with a feeling that we're all part of something. Something that makes sense. Something meaningful . . . And now she prays all the time to see if she can get the feeling back.

Bedouin Where is she now?

Andrew She's currently in a nunnery.

Bedouin Aisha had a similar thing. Couple of years ago. With her it was Zen meditation. Lasted a few months. Just give her space. She'll find what she's looking for.

The Pilot laughs.

Sarah What? What? . . . Say.

Pilot Nothing.

Andrew God. I'm . . . you've had it too. Jesus. I thought I was the only one.

Bedouin No. It's really common.

Andrew It's shit though, isn't it? When it's happening to you. I mean . . . I love her. I don't want her to be a nun.

Bedouin Just . . . stay cool.

Andrew Yeah.

Bedouin Good scene today, I thought.

Andrew I thought so.

Bedouin I love playing a Bedouin. Bedouins are cool as fuck. They've got it sorted. You just need to put this stuff on and you're . . .
    There's a totally natural authority, you know. You just – know.

Andrew I get the same thing in the whole pilot outfit.

The Pilot laughs again.
    Sarah squirms.

Pilot Doesn't matter.

Bedouin Even just then, talking about your wife, you find yourself . . .
    Speaking with authority
    There's a connection to a culture that's a thousand years old, you know. A culture that – it puts things in perspective
    It's – the desert, the desert which is the most hostile environment humans can possibly encounter – and that's where Bedouins live. And it's a spiritual thing

95

Why? Because it's empty. Empty. Silent. And all the time you're on the edge of death. So – all you are – your entire being – becomes alive. Truly alive. What's more spiritual than that – that's a five-star place of contemplation. What I'm saying is – it can't be a coincidence that the world's three great religions – Judaism, Christianity and Islam – they all came from the desert. From the Bedouin.

Andrew I didn't know that.

Bedouin Yeah. 'S true. My theory is that it's to do with simplicity
    The community were nomads but – wherever you go in the desert – it's the same – so 'home' becomes the community plus sand. Two hundred and fifty-six people. A well
    The chief's tent. The women's compound. Order. Sense Meaning. Belonging.

Andrew Yeah. You might be right.

Bedouin You know I'm right. And I'll tell you what. I think that's what Marie's expressing. She's expressing a very deep sense of yearning for the desert. You know. It's a very . . . that's a symptom of our disease. We need more desert.

Andrew Yeah.

Bedouin Let me get you another drink
    . . .
    Listen, Andy – the clapper-loader told me she'd sold you some coke. You don't have any on you, do you?

Andrew Yeah. Sure
    You go on. I'll follow you.

The Bedouin leaves.
    The Pilot has stopped reading.

Sarah So . . . what d'you think?

Pilot Are you serious?

Sarah Tell me.

Pilot OK
I think it's the most ludicrous thing I've ever heard
Firstly – 'The Pilot should enter the plane last. After all
the passengers have boarded.' Who does the pre-flight
checks?

Sarah The co-pilot.

Pilot It's the pilot's responsibility. That's the point. It's his
plane
He's got to check it
'The pilot processes through the cabin at the head of
the stewards and stewardesses in order to be witnessed by
the passengers.' No way
The passengers don't want to see the pilot
The pilot's going to keep them in the air
They want to imagine the pilot. They hear the pilot's
voice on the tannoy, they imagine a man in control. They
see a human and they think – he's just one of us. It's utter
drivel.

Sarah What about the new uniform design?

Pilot Stupid. Pointless.

Sarah The idea is . . . that the naval metaphor doesn't
resonate as strongly as the monarchic metaphor.

Pilot You're in a plane. You want a man who knows.
A man with the hat that says, 'I know.' That's all you
want. Nothing else.

Sarah You didn't like the crown idea?

Pilot The crown idea has no merit in it whatsoever
It's beneath contempt

How did you think it up

What jelly is there inside your head that you think up this stuff? How pointless can an excercise possibly be? Jesus

You're like my daughter

Useless. All over the fucking shop mooning about from half-arsed crisis to half-arsed solution without a single fucking sensible idea in her head. Look at the world. It's a practical place. Jesus. Get a fucking job. Get your hands dirty. This . . . God . . . this . . . world of mental masturbation you live in – learn to fly a fucking plane. Do something. Who gives a shit what the world's like? Live in it. Do the work. Have kids. Pay the mortgage. And get on with it

Don't dwell

Pull yourself together

You make me sick.

Sarah is crying.

Pilot . . .

I'm sorry

I'm sorry . . . you – oh . . .

You said to . . .

Sarah Doesn't matter.

Pilot You said to criticise you.

Sarah Forget it. I'm being silly. I'm being weak. I'm . . .

Pilot You asked . . .

Sarah I'm just . . . God. I'm just . . .

It's the gin. It's the gin

. . .

. . .

The Pilot awkwardly kneels beside her chair.
He holds her.
A little self-consciously.

I'm useless.

Pilot No.

Sarah I am. I'm a waste of space.

Pilot No. You're . . . you're . . .

Sarah I'm a useless piece of shit.

Pilot No
No
You're . . . beautiful. You're beautiful.

Sarah Stay with me.

Pilot I can't. I have to fly to San Diego tonight.

Sarah Stay with me.

Pilot I can't.

Sarah exits.

David Let's go.

*David and Laura exit. Laura limping.
The Mother Superior enters.*

Mother Superior Have you found him, Marie?

Marie No.

Mother Superior Don't worry.

Marie I need him.

Mother Superior I know.

Marie Otherwise what's the point?

Mother Superior Can I let you into a secret?

Marie If you want.

Mother Superior He doesn't exist.

Marie No.

Mother Superior Yeah. I'm afraid so.

Marie But . . .

Mother Superior I know
That's why we have nuns
We pretend
As long as we pretend convincingly, everyone else doesn't have to worry. We mainly do it to humour the priests
But basically. No.

Marie I don't believe you.

Marie exits.

Daniel I didn't come to San Diego to wait for Paul McCartney.

Daniel walks off.

Woman You can't go in through that door.

Daniel Who's behind it?

Woman I can't tell you.

Daniel takes out the knife.

You can't
You can't go in.

Daniel goes in.
Pious follows him.
Darkness.

FIVE

David Greig is sitting at a desk.
Pious and Daniel enter.
David looks up.

Pious Are you Paul McCartney?

David No.

Daniel We should go.

Pious We're looking for Paul McCartney.

David I'm afraid he lives in the the Mull of Kintyre
    Which is well over three thousand miles away from
here
    I tried to bring him over but I wasn't able to.

Pious Do you have his phone number?

David I'm sorry, I don't.

Daniel We should go. Come on, Mum. Let's go.

Pious We're looking for Daniel's mother. All we have is
this postcard. It says she sang backing vocals for Wings.

Pious gives David Greig the postcard.

David I don't know. McCartney definitely went to Lagos.
They recorded in the EMI studios there. It's possible he
heard a woman singing in the marketplace. But she's
certainly not listed on the album. In fact the only Nigerian
who contributed to the album was the recording engineer.
I heard the marketplace story myself when I was living in
Nigeria but I think it's – one of those stories that get told
whenever a global superstar turns up in a third-world
country.

Pious So the postcard is a lie.

David No. It's true. She's not on the album, but she was
on the US tour. McCartney invited her to sing backing
vocals
    She still lives in San Diego. This is the address
    Her name's Patience but she calls herself Amy.

Pious Thank you.

David Don't thank me.

Pious C'mon, Daniel. Now we can find your mother.

Daniel Wait outside, Mum. I want to talk to him.

  Pious leaves.

David I've been wanting to talk to you.

Daniel Why did you bring me here?

David I wanted to get to know you, I suppose.

Daniel It's not possible for you to know me.

David Was it you I saw in London?

Daniel Yes.

David And it was me who threw the acid in your face?

Daniel I don't know. Was it?

David Why did you come to San Diego, Daniel?

Daniel I came to San Diego to kill you.

David I want to –

Daniel I am utterly uninterested in what you want.

David There must be a –

Daniel You are no longer in control
San Diego, from now on
It belongs to me.

  Daniel leaves.
  Darkness.

Act Four

ONE

Pious and Daniel are sitting on the balcony of an
expensive beachfront house in San Diego.
   Marie and Andrew in the desert.
   Andrew dressed as a pilot, Marie dressed as a nun.
   Laura and David on a beach beside a pile of wood
arranged for a bonfire.
   A can of petrol.
   Also a huge pile of meat products.

Andrew I've arranged for you to stay in a Bedouin
encampment
   It's the one we used for filming the last scene
   I thought you'd need some time alone
   But if you need me, the mobile's switched on, and it's
great reception here. They have total coverage
   . . .
   Boy's with the nanny, so happy with the nanny.
Brought you a photo.

   Andrew gives Marie a photo of the boy.

My dad's flying in tonight. I'll probably have a drink with
him. But call – any time – anything.

Marie It's perfect.

Andrew I love you.

Marie It's perfect.

   She kneels and begins to pray.

Andrew So
   You'll be – all right then
   . . .

I love you
OK
I'm thinking of you
OK
Whenever you're ready
I hope you get through to him.

Andrew leaves.

Laura Didn't think we'd get away.

David Plan was bound to work. Plan was genius.

Laura It's cold.

David Yeah. We'll light the fire.

Laura Geese and everything.

David Sodding geese. Would you believe it? You want
them to be there
And there they are
Hundreds of the fuckers.

Laura On their way to Greenland.

David Mad geese cunts.

Laura Don't say that.

David Sorry.

Laura Don't be sorry.

David Sorry.

Laura This is the place, David
We found it
You – and sodding geese – and grey sky and grey sea
And it's a bit cold
It's definitely the place.

David I knew it was.

Laura How did you know?

David I can concentrate when I'm with you
My whole brain – on the one subject
You. And what you want
And I just know
I just completely know what you want
Totally bonkers but it's the truth.

Laura Cocky.

David I am right, Laura. I'm serious.

Laura No joke?

David No joke.

Laura Go on then
What do I want? Right now.

David Oh God

. . .

Laura Go on. What is it.

David I'm embarrassed now.

Laura Tell me.

He suddenly starts to open the packets of meat products.

I want you to cut me.

David You don't.

Laura I do.

David You don't
You want me to need you
And I do. Laura
Without you – I can't concentrate.

Laura I want you to eat me.

David Pretend

From now on. We can pretend.

He gives her a packet of meat product and a knife. She cuts the packet open. She takes out some ham. She gives it to him.

This is you

I'm eating you
All I'm ever going to eat
From now on
Is you.

Patience/Amy enters carrying bottles of beer. She sits. She looks at the postcard.

Patience Jesus. I remember writing this. I was so strung out

During the tour I got badly into drugs and I remember one day this roadie just told me I was fired and I went out, scored, and wrote this to you

Jesus

Different woman. Thank God. Different woman.

Pious You've done very well for yourself in San Diego, Patience.

Patience Actually, do you mind, calling me Amy? It's just – that's who I am now.

Pious Amy.

Amy Amy.

Pious Patience is a good name too.

Amy But Amy's the name I use in San Diego.

Daniel Why did you never come to get me?

Amy Well, son, the thing is at first I had no money

Then, when I set up the massage parlour I started to make some money, I was embarrassed. I didn't want you to see me doing a job like that. So I sent the money for

you to go to school. You know. I thought you were going to school in England. My sister's sister's sister kept sending me letters telling me that you were in England doing your A levels

And then, when I diversified into real estate and I wanted to see you – I wrote and they told me you'd become a lawyer and you didn't really want to get in touch with me because you thought it would upset you in your new life. So I respected that.

Daniel I was in Jos.

Amy I know that now, son
But I didn't know before.

Daniel I looked for you.

Amy I know, son. But look – you can stay with me now. I'll get you enrolled in some adult education classes and you can come work for me. You can stay here, in this house. We'll get to know each other. We'll walk the dogs together. We'll go swimming in the ocean together. We'll talk about old times together

I'll cook Nigerian food for you and it'll be just like we're back on the streets of Lagos

And before you know it, you'll feel at home

When I take people round to buy real estate now – I always say – you'll see many houses – but you'll only ever see one home

When you see it, buy it

This is your home now, son.

Daniel I don't belong here.

Amy Nobody does
Nobody's from here
San Diego is a place people come to.

Daniel I belong under the freeway
I didn't come to San Diego to do adult education courses

It's too late. I don't know you
Come on, Mum. Let's go. We need to scatter Dad's
ashes.

Pious Son.

Daniel I belong with you.

Daniel leaves.

Pious I'm sorry, Amy.

Amy It's OK.

Pious At least – he knows you exist.

Amy I know.

Pious He's very temperamental. Very – he's got a head
full of electricity. But – you'll see. He'll come round.

Amy I feel so responsible.

Pious Don't worry. I'll look after him. He's a good boy.

Amy Thank you.

Pious shakes Amy's hand and leaves.
*David and Laura, lying on the beach, entangled and
enraptured.*

David You see
I knew
I knew, didn't I?

Laura You did.

David And you don't need to cut yourself any more.

Laura No.

David And I can concentrate
As long as you're with me. I can concentrate.

Laura I know.

David And we can pretend. Eat ham with mustard, and Cumberland sausages, and pork chops, and rissoles and mince and . . .
Anything you want.

Laura When I'm with you, I don't feel like like shit.

David That's right.

Laura I know where I'm going
It's in my brain
I know – I can see a direction.

David Yeah.

Laura Like – Greenland – I can see sort of Greenland.

David That's it. That's it.

Laura Dave –

David Yeah.

Laura Dave I've fucked up
I've really fucked up badly.

David No you haven't.

Laura I have
I've done a fucking stupid thing
Really really fucking stupid.

David What?

Laura Before – when you were getting the meat
And – I sat here – and – I saw the geese and everything
And I knew it was the place.

David I told you. Yeah.

Laura I knew it was the place. But I got it wrong about what the place was for
I thought – I did a really stupid thing.

David What?

She shows him an empty bottle of pills.
   Darkness.
   In the darkness.
   A sudden noise in the darkness.

Marie Hello? Is there anybody there? Hello
   Who is it?. . . Andrew?
   . . .
   Hello
   HELLO
   . . .
   I don't have anything
   I have nothing to steal
   . . .
   Go away
   GO AWAY
   Shoo
   Shoo animal shoo
   . . .
   God? . . .

Marie laughs in embarrassment.

. . .

Marie sings.

'Stuck inside these four walls
Oooh
Sent inside together
Ooooh
Never seeing no one nice again like you ooooh
Mama
Yooooh.'

Bright sunshine.
   The Pilot is sitting on the beach, with his trouser
legs rolled up.

Marie is praying. Tired. Very tired.
Laura is almost unconscious on the beach.
David is holding her.
He slaps her. He sticks fingers down her throat. He
pushes her stomach. All in an attempt to make her
vomit.

David Concentrate, David. Fucking concentrate
Jesus. Don't sleep, Laura. Wake up. Concentrate
TELL ME WHAT TO DO.

Laura Sea.

David What? See what? What? Concentrate.
Concentrate.

He thinks, panicking.

Pious and Daniel at the end of the runway. The objects
in front of them.
Pious puts the objects into a plastic bag.

David Concentrate. Think. Think. Concentrate
Geese
Sky
Meat
C'mon
What is it?
Geese
Sky
Meat.

Pious You might as well eat the melon
It'll fill you up
The string. Could be useful. Perhaps you could use it
to tie the bag to your wrist. So you don't drop it when
you run for the plane wheels
The cigarette lighter
Do you smoke?

Daniel No.

Pious Maybe you could use it to keep warm. When you're high up in the atmosphere and it's cold. You could make a small flame
And the notebook
I've written your name in it, and my name and an address where you can get hold of me. And –

The Pilot takes out his mobile phone.

You will write?

Daniel Of course, Mum.

Pious I didn't think I would feel so . . .

Daniel Don't cry. Please don't cry, Mum.

Pious My little goose is leaving the nest.

Daniel I'll be fine.

They embrace.
    The phone beeps to indicate a message is waiting for him.
    The Pilot listens to the message.

Voice First new message
    Received today at 7.21 p.m.
    To listen to the message, press one
    . . .

Laura's Voice Dad
    I'm in Scotland
    I'm at the goose place
    I'm with a boy. And I'm dead happy
    I'm really really happy
    The goose place is where I'm supposed to be
    OK
    So I want you to know
    That I'm sorry

I'm sorry I can't explain better
But – it's OK
Thanks for everything
All right so – bye then
Bye-bye.

Voice To listen to the message again, press one
To delete the message, press two
To call the person who left this message, press three.

The Pilot looks at his watch.
    He decides it is too late to call.

David See what? I can't think. I can't? See what? See
what? Wake up. Wake up.

Voice Message deleted
Next new message
Received today at 11.25 p.m.

Amy's Voice Kevin? It's Amy – remember?
I got your message
I'm at the beach
Why don't you come down to the beach?
Gimme a call when you get there
I'll tell you how to find me
Please come
OK
Bye now.

Pious and Daniel break their embrace.
    The Pilot starts to take his clothes off, down to his shorts.

Pious Take your father. (*He gives Daniel the bag of ashes.*) When the plane is in the air, high up in the jetstream, say a prayer for him and scatter his ashes.

Daniel I will.

Pious And take the knife.

Daniel He didn't want me to have the knife.

Pious I want you to have the knife
   When you get to Nigeria
   Put it in a box and send it to whoever is president with a note telling him to kill himself with it.

Daniel I will.

Pious gives Daniel the knife.
   The Pilot combs his hair and puts his hat on.

David See? Sea. Sea. The sea
   Sea.

He runs to the sea.
   He runs back with a cupped hand full of water.
   She opens her mouth.
   Drinks.
   He runs back.
   Cupped hands.
   Water, mouth drinks.
   Again and again.

Sea.

Laura Sea.

Pious Here is ten dollars
   This is all the money I have
   When you get to Nigeria, write to me with an address
   And I'll send you more money.

Daniel I will.

The Pilot walks towards the sea.
   Amy enters. She is in a bathing suit, with a towel.

Daniel The plane is waiting.

Pious I know.

Daniel I should run.

Pious I know.

David Wake up. Wake up.

Laura Sea
I feel sick.

David Sick
Seasick. Concentrate
Wake up. Wake up.

Laura's eyes open.
She looks at him.

Laura It's all right.

Daniel Good bye, Mum.

Pious Be safe.

Amy and the Pilot walk into the sea holding hands.
Daniel suddenly runs.
The noise of a plane about to land.
Laura pukes. At first dry, then vomits. David holds
her as she vomits and vomits until eventually, a small
posset of pills is vomited up.
The huge sound of the plane as it is right overhead.
Pious kneels to pray.
Pious looks up at the aeroplane.
Marie opens her eyes.
The wind blows.

David Thank God
Thank you God
Thank God.

The bump and screech of a plane landing.
The reverse thrust of the engines.
The noise quiets.
Darkness.
In the darkness.
The Pilot's voice.

Pilot Ladies and gentlemen, welcome to San Diego, we hope you've enjoyed flying with us today. The temperature outside is a rather warm 82 degrees and the local time is 3.37 p.m.

Thanks once again for flying with us and we hope you'll fly with us again soon.

. . .

Cabin crew, door to manual.

The End.